Laboratory Manual
to accompany

¿QUÉ TAL?
AN INTRODUCTORY COURSE • THIRD EDITION

María Sabló-Yates
Delta College

McGraw-Hill, Inc.
New York St. Louis San Francisco Auckland Bogotá
Caracas Lisbon London Madrid Mexico Milan
Montreal New Delhi Paris San Juan Singapore
Sydney Tokyo Toronto

This is an ⌐B⌐ book.

Laboratory Manual to accompany *¿Qué tal? An Introductory Course*

4 5 6 7 8 9 0   MAL   MAL   9 0 9 8 7 6 5 4 3 2

ISBN: 0-07-557423-3

Manufactured in the United States of America

Word Processing: Fog Press
Illustrators: Katherine Tillotson, Axelle Fortier, Judith Macdonald

Grateful acknowledgment is made for use of the following:
Realia
Page 31 © *Diario de Juarez,* Editora Paso del Norte; *45* © Antonio Mingote; *75* ©
Quino; *133* © Quino; *161* © Antonio Mingote; *179* © Antonio Mingote; *188* © Quino;
192 © Alt; *214* © Quino.

Contents

To Instructors and Students

The third edition of the tape program to accompany *¿Qué tal?* contains a variety of exercises to help students practice listening to, speaking, reading, writing, and, above all, understanding the Spanish language. In this edition there is an increased emphasis on contextualized practice, functional language usage, and cultural content, as well as more types of listening comprehension activities, including exercises based on realia (real things, such as advertisements, classified ads, cartoons and so on, that one encounters in a Spanish-speaking country) and exercises in which students interact with the speakers on the tape.

In addition to these types of exercises, the third edition of the *¿Qué tal?* tape program introduces other new features. New to this edition is a section called **Estrategias** that introduces and practices a variety of listening strategies: techniques that improve one's ability to understand spoken Spanish. Another new feature is the option of writing some answers to the interviews (**Entrevistas**). This gives instructors some flexibility in checking answers as well as evaluating writing. Since writing the answers is an option only, students should ask their instructor how this specific type of exercise should be handled.

The tape program follows the format of individual chapters in the text. Each chapter begins with a vocabulary section (**Vocabulario**). The first part of this section is followed by pronunciation and spelling exercises (**Pronunciación y ortografía**), the minidialogues from the text, then exercises and activities on the grammatical concepts of the chapter (**Estructuras**). Most chapters have a **Vocabulario** section in the middle, following the text's format. Chapter vocabulary and grammar are combined in **Un poco de todo** sections. Alternating **Un poco de todo** sections introduce and practice listening strategies (**Estrategias**). Finally, as in the text, alternating chapters end with functional dialogue practice (**Un paso más: Situaciones**). Exercises and activities in most sections progress from controlled to more open-ended and personalized or interactive, to give students the chance to be creative in Spanish as well as to practice specific vocabulary and structures.

As in the textbook, there are additional review sections (**Repasos**) after chapters 4, 8, 12, 16, 20, and 24. We have made an effort to reintroduce vocabulary and grammar from previous chapters in these review sections and throughout the Laboratory Manual, so that students have the opportunity to use the grammatical structures and vocabulary they have learned in a variety of contexts. In addition, the **Repaso** sections contain a review of the listening strategies practiced in previous **Estrategias** sections.

Although the tape program includes some material taken directly from *¿Qué tal?*, it also contains much that is totally new: contextualized exercises (including question-and-answer sequences and interviews) dictations, personalized questions, visually based listening comprehension exercises, cultural listening passages (in the **Un poco de todo** and **Repaso** sections), activities based on realia, additional brief dialogues, some interactive in nature and— beginning in **Capítulo 19**—songs.

The following types of exercises are a regular feature of the *¿Qué tal?* tape program and can be found in most chapters.

- **Definiciones**, **Situaciones**, and **Asociaciones** use a multiple choice or matching format in order to test listening comprehension and vocabulary. **Identificaciones** and **Descripción**, as their names imply, ask students to generate responses based on visuals, with or without written or oral cues. Although these are more controlled in nature, they are all contextualized and related to the theme of the current or a previous chapter. Answers to these types of exercises are given immediately after each item or at the end of the sequence, and time is allowed for repetition of the correct answer. In this way, students know immediately if they have understood the exercise.
- **Conversación** is the title for the functional minidialogues taken from the text and any other conversation in which students take the role of one of the speakers after listening to the model conversation. At times students answer by using cues that are in the manual; on other occasions personal experience is the only guide. The **Conversación** dialogues give students a chance to engage in everyday types of conversations. It may be appropriate to have students record answers to these activities, if your language laboratory has the required capability.
- There are two types of question-and-answer sequences, **Preguntas** and **Entrevista**. **Preguntas** are more controlled in that an oral or written cue is given. The correct answer is heard on the tape after each item. The **Entrevistas**, on the other hand, are more open-ended and personalized. They give practice in answering as well as asking questions. They usually appear at the end of a grammar section or in the **Un poco de todo** or **Repaso** sections, and they recombine vocabulary and grammar from the current chapter or previous chapters. Although possible answers are given for some of the **Entrevista** exercises, many do not offer responses. An instructor may want students to record their answers so that he or she can listen to them later. As noted earlier, there is also the option of stopping the tape and writing answers to these exercises. We believe that this feature offers instructors some flexibility without altering the listening comprehension-based nature of the tape program.
- Although the entire lab program is in effect listening comprehension practice, specific listening strategies can be found in the section called **Estrategias**. Some of the strategies included gisting, listening for specific information, and recognizing cognate, suffix, and prefix patterns. In these sections, students practice ways to decode what they hear. Answers are given immediately after each sequence or after each item in the exercise.
- Culturally-based listening passages are found in alternating chapters. These are brief paragraphs that develop the theme of the chapter and offer cultural insights. The comprehension questions that follow are usually multiple choice or true/false. No answers are given on the tape.
- The Laboratory Manual also includes many types of dictations (**Dictados**) in which students are asked to listen for and write down specific letters, words, phrases, or entire sentences. One variation of the dictation format involves listening to a conversation or series of brief conversations and writing down a list of requested information. Students' ability to listen for specific information in Spanish will be enhanced by these types of exercises.

In the Laboratory Manual itself, you will find the exercises for the pronunciation sections, model sentences for most vocabulary and grammar exercises, visuals on which activities are based, the text of most of the **Conversación** dialogues, and the words to the songs. The text for the minidialogues, the listening passages, and other listening comprehension exercises is not provided in the Laboratory Manual, since these are offered for listening comprehension practice.

Visuals are used to illustrate and provide a context for the minidialogues. There are also a number of visually based activities. Time is provided on the tape to scan the drawings, but the stop-the-tape option should be used, if possible, to give more time to "look" if needed. Sound effects are used throughout the tape program, when appropriate. A variety of native speakers appear so that students can get used to the variety of accents and voice types found in the Spanish-speaking world, but no accent will be so pronounced as to be difficult to understand. In most parts of the tape program, speakers will speak at a natural or close to natural speed (particularly in exercises for which the text is provided in the manual).

We hope that the changes in format and content will provide a natural context within which students and instructors alike will enjoy working with Spanish.

This Laboratory Manual and tape program would not have been possible without the help and editing of Thalia Dorwick, whose patience and support over the years have been invaluable. We also offer our sincere thanks to Marc Accornero, whose voice is heard on the songs and who was instrumental in their selection, and to Ron, Jonathan, and Catherine Yates and to Duquesne Sabló for their constant support and understanding throughout the writing process.

María Sabló-Yates
November 8, 1990

PASOS PRELIMINARES

Paso uno

Saludos y expresiones de cortesía

A. *Diálogos.* In the following dialogues, you will practice greeting others appropriately in Spanish. The dialogues will be read with pauses for repetition. After each dialogue, you will hear summarizing statements. Circle the letter of the statement that best describes each dialogue. First, listen.

1. ANA: Hola, José.
    JOSÉ: ¿Qué tal, Ana?
    ANA: Así así. ¿Y tú?
    JOSÉ: ¡Muy bien! Hasta mañana, ¿eh?
    ANA: Adiós.

Comprensión: a   b

2. SEÑOR ALONSO: Buenas tardes, señorita López.
    SEÑORITA LÓPEZ: Muy buenas, señor Alonso. ¿Cómo está?
    SEÑOR ALONSO: Bien, gracias. ¿Y usted?
    SEÑORITA LÓPEZ: Muy bien, gracias. Adiós.
    SEÑOR ALONSO: Hasta luego.

Comprensión: a   b

3. MARÍA: Buenos días, profesora.
    PROFESORA: Buenos días. ¿Cómo se llama usted?
    MARÍA: Me llamo María Sánchez.
    PROFESORA: Mucho gusto.
    MARÍA: Encantada.

Comprensión: a   b

B. *Otros saludos y expresiones de cortesía.* Repeat the following sentences, imitating the speaker.

1. ¿Cómo estás, Alberto?
2. ¿Cómo te llamas?
3. Encantada, señorita.
4. Muchas gracias, Juan.
5. De nada, Elena.
6. Con permiso, señora.
7. ¡Perdón!
8. Por favor, Ana...
9. Buenas noches, Julio.

C. *¿Qué dicen estas personas?* (What are these people saying?) Circle the letter of the drawing that is best described by the sentences you hear. Each will be said twice.

1. a)    b)

2. a)    b)

3. a)    b)

4. a)    b)

D. *Situaciones.* You will hear a series of questions or statements. Give an appropriate response for each. The answer you hear is not the only possible answer, but repeat it anyway after you hear it!

1. ...   2. ...   3. ...   4. ...   5. ...   6. ...

Pronunciación y ortografía: El alfabeto español

A. You will hear the names of the letters in the Spanish alphabet, along with a list of place names. Listen and repeat, imitating the speaker. Notice that most Spanish consonants are pronounced differently than in English. In future chapters, you will have a chance to practice the pronunciation of most of these letters individually.

a	**a**	la Argentina	**n**	**ene**	Nicaragua
b	**be**	Bolivia	**ñ**	**eñe**	España
c	**ce**	Cáceres	**o**	**o**	Oviedo
ch	**che**	Chile	**p**	**pe**	Panamá
d	**de**	Durango	**qu**	**cu**	Quito
e	**e**	el Ecuador	**r**	**ere**	el Perú
f	**efe**	la Florida	**rr**	**erre**	Monterrey
g	**ge**	Guatemala	**s**	**ese**	San Juan
h	**hache**	Honduras	**t**	**te**	Toledo
i	**i**	Ibiza	**u**	**u**	el Uruguay
j	**jota**	Jalisco	**v**	**ve**	Venezuela
k	**ca**	(*Kansas*)	**w**	**doble ve**	(*Washington*)
l	**ele**	Lima	**x**	**equis**	Extremadura
ll	**elle**	Sevilla	**y**	**i griega**	el Paraguay
m	**eme**	México	**z**	**zeta**	Zaragoza

B. Repeat the following words, imitating the speaker and paying close attention to the difference in pronunciation between Spanish and English.

1. **j**   José   julio   Jamaica   Jiménez
2. **h**   hotel   Héctor   La Habana   historia
3. **ñ**   La Coruña   cabaña   señor   niña
4. **ll, y**   Castilla   cordillera   Yolanda   yate
5. **g**   agua   Guillermo   Germán   gitano
6. **c**   Caracas   Colón   César   Cecilia

C. You will hear a series of words. Each will be said twice. Circle the Spanish consonant used to spell each word.

1. l   ll   3. h   j   5. j   g
2. n   ñ   4. b   g   6. c   ch

Los cognados

A. Repeat the following cognates, imitating the speaker.

1. cruel   5. tímido   8. religioso
2. idealista   6. introvertido   9. emocional
3. paciente   7. terrible   10. seria
4. generosa

B. *Estrategias: Cognates.* As you know, Spanish and English share a large number of cognates. Being able to recognize cognates will make it possible for you to understand a good deal of what you hear and read in Spanish as well as increase your Spanish vocabulary.

It is often easier to recognize a cognate in written form than when it is said. With practice, you will learn to identify many cognates when you hear them. In the following exercise, you will hear as well as say some cognates.

¿Quiere aprender un idioma extranjero? (Do you want to learn a foreign language?) Listen to the following ad for foreign-language classes given by *Idiomas Serrano*. It is from a Spanish newspaper. Then try to find the Spanish equivalent of the following English words. (Remember to repeat the answer.)

1. methodology
2. native
3. audiovisual
4. modern
5. technique

C. *Dictado:* * ¿*Cómo son?* (What are they like?) You will hear five sentences. Each will be said twice. Listen carefully and write the missing words.

1. Nicolás es _____. 4. Maite es muy _____.

2. La profesora Díaz es _____. 5. Íñigo no es _____.

3. Don Juan no es _____.

¿Cómo es usted?

A. *Descripción*. Describe these people, using the written and oral cues. (Remember to repeat the correct answer.)

MODELO: Juan (optimista) → <u>Juan es optimista</u>.

1. yo 3. tú
2. Cecilia 4. Luis

B. *¿Cómo es usted?* What kind of person are you? Describe yourself, using the oral cues. Remember that if you are female, the final -o must be changed to -a. The answer you will hear is not the only possible answer. (Remember to repeat the answer.)

MODELO: (generoso) → <u>Soy generosa</u> or <u>No soy generosa</u>.

1. ... 2. ... 3. ... 4. ... 5. ...

C. *Preguntas*. Ask the following persons about their personalities, using ¿**eres...** ? or ¿**es usted...** ?, as appropriate, and the cues you will hear. Follow the model. (Remember to repeat the answer. Or, if you prefer, stop the tape and write the answer.)

MODELO: Marta (tímida) → Marta, ¿<u>eres tímida?</u>

1. Ramón, _____

2. Señora Alba., _____

_____

* Answers to all *Dictado* exercises are given in the Appendix.

3. Señor Moreno, _____

4. Anita, _____

Paso dos
Más cognados

A. *Descripción.* In this exercise, you will practice gisting, that is, getting the main idea, an important skill in language learning. Although some of the vocabulary you hear will not be familiar to you, concentrate on the words that you *do* know and listen for cognates. After the exercise, you will be asked to choose the statement that best describes the passage.

1   2

B. *Dictado: Asociaciones.* For each of the following categories, you will hear a series of three words. Each series will be said twice. Write only the word or words you associate with each category. In this exercise, you will practice listening for specific information.

1. Naciones: _____

2. Instrumentos musicales: _____

3. Personas: _____

4. Animales: _____

5. Cosas (*Things*): _____

C. *¿Qué es esto?* (What is this?) You will hear a series of cognates. Each will be said twice. Repeat each one, telling in what category it belongs. First, listen to the list of categories.

un lugar (*a place*)   una bebida (*a drink*)
un deporte (*a sport*)   un animal
un instrumento musical   un concepto

    MODELO: (¿Qué es un rancho?) → <u>Es un lugar</u>.

1. ...   2. ...   3. ...   4. ...   5. ...   6. ...

Pronunciación y ortografía—Las vocales—*A, E, I, O, U*

A. Repeat the following pairs of Spanish and English words, imitating the speaker. Note that Spanish vowels are short and tense; they are never drawn out with a *u* or an *i* glide as in English.

say / se   *tee* / ti   *low* / lo   *to* / tú

say / se   *tee* / ti   *low* / lo   *to* / tú

B. Repeat the following Spanish syllables, imitating the speaker. Try to pronounce each vowel with a short, tense sound.

1. ma   fa   la   ta   pa   4. mo   fo   lo   to   po
2. me   fe   le   te   pe   5. mu   fu   lu   tu   pu
3. mi   fi   li   ti   pi

C. Repeat the following words, imitating the speaker. Be careful to avoid the English schwa, the "uh" sound. Remember to pronounce each vowel with a short and tense sound.

1. hasta   tal   nada   mañana   natural
2. me   qué   Pérez   usted   rebelde
3. así   señorita   permiso   imposible   tímido
4. yo   con   cómo   noches   profesor
5. uno   tú   mucho   Perú   Lupe

D. *Dictado*. Listen carefully to the following words. Each will be said twice. Write the missing vowels.

1. p___s___   4. c___n___

2. c___s___   5. p___s___r

3. m___s___   6. m___s___

Los números 0–30

A. *Las bolsas* (money exchanges) *internacionales*. You will hear a series of numbers from the following chart. Each will be said twice. Circle the number you hear and repeat each number. The word *coma* means comma; it is used instead of the decimal point in many Hispanic countries. In this exercise, you will practice listening for specific information.

Indicadores de Bolsas Internacionales	
País	
USA	7,2
Japón	14,4
Alemania	5,6
Francia	6,2
R. Unido	8,0
Holanda	4,3
Suiza	7,0
Suecia	7,8
Italia	6,3
España	4,1

B. *¿Cuánto es?* (How much does it cost?) You will hear the price of three different brands of items you want to purchase. Repeat the price of the most expensive brand. In this exercise, you will practice listening for specific information. (Remember to repeat the answer.)

1. ...   2. ...   3. ...   4. ...

C. *Dictado.* You will hear eight numbers. Each will be said twice. Write out the number you hear in the corresponding place.

6 _____   0 _____

13 _____   3 _____

24 _____   28 _____

2 _____   12 _____

D. *¿Qué hay en la sala de clase?* (What is there in the classroom?) You will hear a series of questions. Each will be said twice. Answer based on the following drawing. (Remember to repeat the answers.)

1. ...   2. ...   3. ...   4. ...

Gustos y preferencias

A. *Preguntas.* Ask a friend whether he or she likes the items mentioned in the cues you will hear.

     MODELO: (la universidad) → ¿Te gusta la universidad?

1. ...   2. ...   3. ...   4. ...   5. ...

B. *¿Qué te gusta?* (What do you like?) Listen to the following conversation about preferences.

     —¿Te gusta el béisbol?
     —Sí, me gusta, pero (*but*) me gusta más (*more*) el vólibol.

Now you will hear a series of questions. Each will be said twice. Answer them, following the model of the conversation you have just heard and using the written cues. (Remember to repeat the answer.)

1. Sí,... / tocar (*to play*) el violín
2. Sí,... / la música popular
3. Sí,... / el tenis
4. Sí,... / beber (*to drink*) café

C. *Entrevista.* You will hear four questions about your likes and dislikes. Each will be said twice. Answer based on your own preferences. You will hear a possible answer on the tape. (Remember to repeat the answer. Or, if you prefer, stop the tape and write the answer.)

1. _____
2. _____
3. _____
4. _____

Paso tres

¿Qué hora es?

A. *¿Qué hora es?* Answer according to the drawings after you hear the corresponding number.

1.  2.  3.

4.  5.   6.

B. *¿A qué hora es... ?* You will hear a series of brief conversations about what time some events take place. Circle the letter of the clock face that shows the time mentioned for each event.

MODELO: ¿A qué hora es la excursión? —A las diez de la mañana.

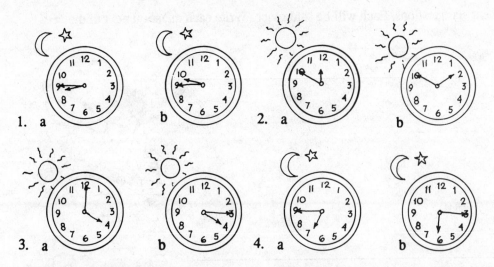

1. a   b   2. a   b

3. a   b   4. a   b

C. *Entrevista.* You will hear a series of questions. Each will be said twice. Answer based on your own experience. You will hear a possible answer on the tape. First, listen to some words that may help you answer some of the questions. (Remember to repeat the answer. Or, if you prefer, stop the tape and write the answer.)

mirar (*to watch*)   estudiar (*to study*)   almorzar (*to have lunch*)

1. _____

2. _____

3. _____

4. _____

5. _____

Las palabras interrogativas: Un resumen

A. *Preguntas.* Your friend Antonio has just made some statements that you didn't quite understand. You will hear each statement twice. Indicate the interrogative word or phrase you should use to obtain information about what he said.

1. a) ¿cuándo?   b) ¿cuánto?
2. a) ¿cómo es?   b) ¿dónde?
3. a) ¿cuántos?   b) ¿dónde?
4. a) ¿cuántos?   b) ¿a qué hora?
5. a) ¿qué es?   b) ¿cómo está?
6. a) ¿cuál?   b) ¿a qué hora?

B. *Dictado.* You will hear six questions. Each will be said twice. Write each question next to the appropriate drawing.

1. _____

2. _____

3. _____

4. _____

5. _____

6. _____

Mandatos y frases comunes en la clase

A. Repeat the following sentences, imitating the speaker.

1. Otra vez, por favor.
2. No entiendo.
3. Tengo una pregunta.

4. No sé la respuesta.
5. Sí, cómo no.
6. Espere un momento, por favor.

B. *¿Qué acaba de decir el profesor?* (What did the professor just say?) The following drawings show a classroom in which a professor has just given several commands. You will hear each of his commands twice. Write the number of each command next to the corresponding drawing.

a. ___

b. ___

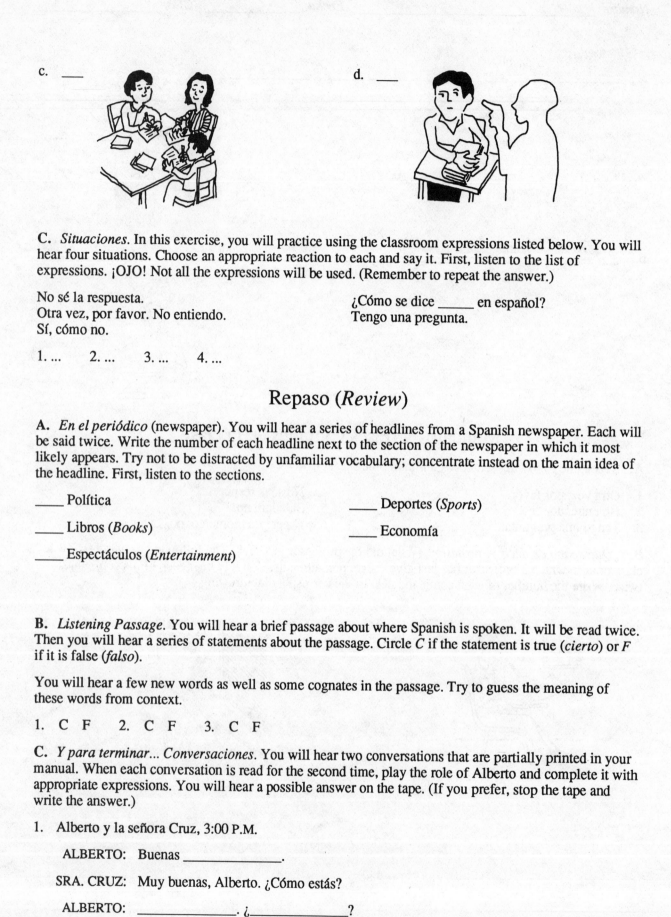

c. ___

d. ___

C. *Situaciones*. In this exercise, you will practice using the classroom expressions listed below. You will hear four situations. Choose an appropriate reaction to each and say it. First, listen to the list of expressions. ¡OJO! Not all the expressions will be used. (Remember to repeat the answer.)

No sé la respuesta.
Otra vez, por favor. No entiendo.
Sí, cómo no.

¿Cómo se dice _____ en español?
Tengo una pregunta.

1. ...   2. ...   3. ...   4. ...

Repaso (*Review*)

A. *En el periódico* (newspaper). You will hear a series of headlines from a Spanish newspaper. Each will be said twice. Write the number of each headline next to the section of the newspaper in which it most likely appears. Try not to be distracted by unfamiliar vocabulary; concentrate instead on the main idea of the headline. First, listen to the sections.

_____ Política

_____ Libros (*Books*)

_____ Espectáculos (*Entertainment*)

_____ Deportes (*Sports*)

_____ Economía

B. *Listening Passage*. You will hear a brief passage about where Spanish is spoken. It will be read twice. Then you will hear a series of statements about the passage. Circle *C* if the statement is true (*cierto*) or *F* if it is false (*falso*).

You will hear a few new words as well as some cognates in the passage. Try to guess the meaning of these words from context.

1. C F   2. C F   3. C F

C. *Y para terminar... Conversaciones*. You will hear two conversations that are partially printed in your manual. When each conversation is read for the second time, play the role of Alberto and complete it with appropriate expressions. You will hear a possible answer on the tape. (If you prefer, stop the tape and write the answer.)

1. Alberto y la señora Cruz, 3:00 P.M.

    ALBERTO: Buenas _____.

    SRA. CRUZ: Muy buenas, Alberto. ¿Cómo estás?

    ALBERTO: _____. ¿_____?

SRA. CRUZ: Muy bien, gracias. Hasta luego, Alberto.

ALBERTO: _____.

2. Alberto y Susana, estudiantes, 9:00 A.M.

SUSANA: Buenos días. ¿Cómo te llamas?

ALBERTO: _____. _____. ¿_____?

SUSANA: Me llamo Susana.

ALBERTO: _____.

SUSANA: Encantada, Alberto.

CAPÍTULO

I

Vocabulario: Escenas universitarias

A. *Asociaciones.* A friend is describing a series of locations. Try to guess the locations he is describing. Write the number of the description next to the location. In this exercise, you will practice getting the general idea in spite of unfamiliar vocabulary. First, listen to the list of locations.

_____ un cuarto (*room*) en la residencia _____ una biblioteca

_____ una oficina _____ una sala de clase

B. *Identificaciones.* You will hear a series of sentences that describe the items in the drawing. Give the number that corresponds to each identification; then repeat the sentence. First, look at the drawing. (Remember to repeat the answer.)

1. ...   2. ...   3. ...   4. ...   5. ...   6. ...   7. ...   8. ...   9. ...   10. ...

C. *¿Es hombre o mujer* (man or woman)? You will hear a series of nouns that refer to people. Identify each by telling whether the person is male or female. In this exercise, you will practice listening for specific information—here, the definite article and the noun ending to determine gender. (Remember to repeat the answer.)

MODELO: (¿La profesora?) → <u>Es mujer</u>.

1. ...   2. ...   3. ...   4. ...   5. ...

Pronunciación y ortografía: Diphthongs and Linking

A. Repeat the following words, paying close attention to the pronunciation of the indicated vowels.

Weak vowels:

(i) Pili   jirafa   oficina   presidente

(u) gusto   lugar   Cuba   universidad

Strong vowels:

(a) Ana   nada   patata   calabaza

(e) trece   elefante   clase   general

(o) los   dólar   profesor   político

B. Diphthongs are formed by two successive weak vowels (*i* or *y, u*) or by a combination of a weak vowel and a strong vowel (*a, e, o*). The two vowels are pronounced as a single syllable. Repeat the following words containing diphthongs.

1. **(ia)**   residencia   gracias
2. **(ie)**   bien   siete
3. **(io)**   Julio   adiós
4. **(iu)**   ciudad (*city*)   viuda (*widow*)
5. **(oi)**   soy   estoy
6. **(ua)**   Eduardo   Managua
7. **(ue)**   buenos   nueve
8. **(uo)**   cuota   arduo
9. **(au)**   auto   aumentar
10. **(eu)**   Ceuta   deuda (*debt*)
11. **(ai)**   aire   hay
12. **(ui)**   ¡cuidado! (*careful!*)   fui (*I was/went*)
13. **(ei)**   veinte   treinta

C. Diphthongs can occur within a word or between words, causing the words to be "linked" and pronounced as one long word. Repeat the following phrases, imitating the speaker.

1. **(oi/ia)**   Armando y Alicia   las letras o y hache
2. **(ei/ie)**   el tigre y el chimpancé   veinte y siete
3. **(ai/iu)**   Elena y Humberto   la silla y un libro

D. Linking also occurs naturally between many word boundaries in Spanish. Repeat the following sentences and phrases, saying each without pause as if it were one long word.

1. ¿Dónde hay un escritorio?
2. tu auto y un estéreo
3. Tomás y Alicia
4. la Argentina y el Uruguay
5. Colorado y Arizona
6. la oficina en el edificio

E. *Dictado.* You will hear four sentences. Each will be said twice. Listen carefully and write what you hear.

1. _____

2. _____

3. _____

4. _____

Estructuras

1. Identifying People and Things: Singular Nouns; Gender and Articles

A. *Minidiálogo: En la clase: El primer día.* You will hear a dialogue followed by a series of statements about the dialogue. Circle *C* if the statement is true (*cierto*) or *F* if it is false (*falso*). In this exercise, you will practice listening for specific information.

1. C F   2. C F   3. C F

B. *¿Qué te gusta?* Tell a friend what you like, using the oral cues and the correct definite article. (Remember to repeat the answer.)

MODELO: (librería) → Me gusta <u>la librería</u>.

1. ...   2. ...   3. ...   4. ...   5. ...

C. *¿Qué hay en el cuarto* (room)? Identify the items in the room after you hear the corresponding number. Begin each sentence with **Hay un...** or **Hay una...** (Remember to repeat the answer.)

D. *Dictado: ¿Quién? ¿Dónde? ¿Qué?* You will hear a series of words. Each will be said twice. Repeat each word and write it in the appropriate category.

PERSONAS	EDIFICIOS O LUGARES	COSAS
_____	_____	_____
_____	_____	_____
_____	_____	_____

Estructuras

2. Identifying People and Things: Nouns and Articles; Plural Forms

A. *Dictado: Escenas de la universidad: Una oficina desordenada* (messy). You will hear a brief description of Professor Adán's office. It will be read twice. Write the names of the objects in his office, in the appropriate column, singular or plural. The articles are given for you.

SINGULAR	PLURAL
el _____	unos _____
un _____	unos _____
un _____	las _____
	unos _____

B. You will hear a series of phrases. Give the plural form of the first four nouns and articles and the singular form of the next four. (Remember to repeat the correct answer.)

Singular → plural

1. ...   2. ...   3. ...   4. ...

Plural → singular

5. ...   6. ...   7. ...   8. ...

C. *Identificaciones.* You will hear a series of words. Each will be said twice. Circle the letter of the person or persons to whom the words might refer. In this exercise you will need to listen carefully to the endings of the words you hear.

1. a) María y Teresa   b) la señorita Rojas
2. a) Luisa y Ana   b) Tomás y Carolina
3. a) Alberto   b) Ángela
4. a) los profesores   b) las mujeres

D. *Los errores de Pablo.* You will hear some statements that your friend Pablo makes about the following drawing. He is wrong and you must correct him. (Remember to repeat the answer.)

MODELO: (Hay dos libros.) → <u>No. Hay tres libros</u>.

Un poco de todo

A. *Asociaciones.* Tell whether the nouns you will hear might be found in the places indicated in your manual. Use the expressions **¡creo que sí!** (*I think so!*) and **¡creo que no!** (*I don't think so!*). You will hear a possible answer on the tape.

MODELO: una cafetería (exámenes) →<u>¡Creo que no! No hay exámenes en una cafetería</u>.

1. una oficina
2. una biblioteca
3. un edificio

4. un cuarto de la residencia
5. una clase

B. *Estrategias: Guessing Words from Context.* Most of the listening activities you have done so far have primarily contained vocabulary that is already familiar to you because it is the active vocabulary of the current or previous chapters. In "real life" listening situations, however, you will definitely encounter more unfamiliar than familiar words.

In the next few chapters of this manual, you will practice guessing the meaning of unfamiliar words from context. It is definitely more difficult to do this in a listening situation than in reading! It will help to pay close attention to the words that surround the unknown vocabulary as well as to the position of the unfamiliar word in the sentences. For example: In the sentence **Marcos trabaja en la biblioteca,** it is safe to guess that **trabaja** is a verb; that is, Marcos does something in the library.

Listen to the following sentences and brief dialogue and circle the verbs.

1. Los niños juegan al básquetbol en el parque.
2. Luisa come en un restaurante cubano.
3. —¿Cuántas personas trabajan en la oficina?
   —Bueno, tres secretarios y una jefa.
   —¿Y quién es la jefa?
   —Es la señora Martínez Hurtado.

Now listen to the sentences again and circle the letter of the probable meaning of indicated words. Try not to look back at the sentences in your manual.

1. In **Los niños juegan al básquetbol, juegan** probably means:
   a) play   b) run   c) live
2. The verb **come** might mean:
   a) sleeps   b) owns   c) eats
3. The verb **trabajan** probably means:
   a) argue   b) work   c) speak
4. The word **jefa** probably refers to:
   a) an object   b) a person   c) a part of the office
5. **Jefa** probably means:
   a) window   b) typewriter   c) boss

C. *Y para terminar... Entrevista.* You will hear a series of questions about your Spanish class and your university. Each will be said twice. Answer based on your own experience. You will hear a possible answer on the tape. The word **su** means *your*. (If you prefer, stop the tape and write the answer.)

1. _____

2. _____

3. _____

4. _____

5. _____

CAPÍTULO

2

Vocabulario: Las materias

A. *En la biblioteca.* You work at the reserve desk at the library, and you are organizing the books for this semester. Which books correspond to which classes? You will hear the names of the books twice. Circle the letter of the most appropriate choice. In this exercise you will practice listening for cognates.

1. a) Es para una clase de matemáticas.   b) Es para una clase de sicología.

2. a) Es para una clase de comercio.   b) Es para una clase de inglés

3. a) Es para una clase de español.   b) Es para una clase de ciencias naturales.

4. a) Es para una clase de computación.   b) Es para una clase de historia.

B. *¿Qué estudian?* You will hear a brief paragraph about what Raquel and Fernando study. It will be said twice. Listen carefully and circle the names of the subjects that each person studies. In this exercise, you will practice listening for specific information. The word **facultad** means school or division, as in Law School or Humanities Division.

Raquel estudia... física   anatomía   computación   sicología   biología

Fernando estudia... español   ciencias   políticas   comercio   biología   inglés   geografía   historia

C. *Hablando de estudios.* (Talking about studies.) The following ads for courses appeared in various Hispanic newspapers. Glance at them and decide which course or courses each of the people described on the tape should take. First, skim the ads, focusing on cognates and key phrases. (You have fifteen seconds to look at the ads. Begin now.)

a)

b)

c)

Mercedes:___

Tina:___

Pablo:___

Pronunciación y ortografía: Stress and Written Accent Marks

A. Repeat the following words, imitating the speaker. The italicized syllable receives the stress in pronunciation.

> • If a word ends in a vowel, *n*, or *s*, stress normally falls on the next-to-the-last syllable.
> *Ti*to *si*lla e*xa*men b*ue*nos
> • If a word ends in any other consonant, stress normally falls on the last syllable.
> particu*lar* libe*ral* universi*dad* profe*sor*
> • Any exception to these two rules will have a written accent mark on the stressed vowel.
> a*diós* Ra*món* fran*cés* *Gó*mez mate*má*ticas sim*pá*tico

B. In words containing diphthongs, a written accent on the weak vowel will break the diphthong, causing it to be pronounced as two separate syllables. Two strong vowels together also result in two separate syllables. Repeat the following words, imitating the speaker.

1. dí-a   Marí-a
2. rí-o (*river*) tí-o
3. con-ti-nú-e   gra-dú-e
4. a-e-ro-puer-to   a-or-ta   bo-a   re-or-ga-ni-zar

C. *Dictado.* You will hear the following words. Each will be said twice. Listen carefully and write in a written accent where required.

1. papa
2. musica
3. practico
4. nacion
5. doctor
6. Maria
7. joven
8. inteligente
9. biologia

Estructuras

3. Expressing Actions: Subject Pronouns; Present Tense of *-ar* verb; Negation

A. *Minidiálogo: Una fiesta para los estudiantes extranjeros.* You will hear a dialogue followed by a series of statements about the dialogue. Circle *C* if the statement is true (*cierto*) or *F* if it is false (*falso*). In this exercise, you will practice listening for specific information.

1. C F   2. C F   3. C F

B. *¿Quién habla?* Answer the questions according to the model. You will be using subject pronouns for emphasis.

MODELO: (¿Quién? ¿Ud?) → <u>Sí, yo hablo</u>.

1. ...   2. ...   3. ...   4. ...   5. ...   6. ...

C. *Dictado: Mi amiga y yo.* You will hear the speaker make a series of statements about herself and a friend. Each will be said twice. Listen carefully and write the verb forms you hear next to the correct subject pronoun. ¡OJO! Remember that subject pronouns are not always used in Spanish and that the verb ending will tell you who the subject is. The word **juntas** means together.

ella:_____

nosotras:_____, _____

yo:_____ , _____

D. *Mis compañeros y yo.* Practice telling about yourself and others, using the oral and written cues. Do not repeat the subject pronouns unless they are needed. (Remember to repeat the answer.)

MODELO: estudiar español (yo) → Estudio español.

1. pagar la matrícula
2. regresar a la biblioteca
3. hablar bien el español
4. desear tomar inglés

5. enseñar muy bien
6. no estudiar mucho
7. necesitar comprar libros
8. trabajar en la cafetería

E. *Entrevista.* You are a new student at this university, and some recent acquaintances are asking you about your life on campus. You will hear each question twice. Answer the questions according to your own experience. You will hear a possible answer on the tape. (If you prefer, stop the tape and write the answer.)

1. _____

2. _____

3. _____

4. Sí, (No, no) quiero _____

5. Prefiero _____

6. _____

Estructuras

4.   Getting Information: Asking Yes/No Questions

A. *Minidiálogo: En una universidad: La oficina de matrícula.* You will hear a dialogue followed by a series of statements. Circle the letter of the person who might have made each statement. In this exercise, you will practice listening for specific information.

1. a) la estudiante
2. a) la estudiante
3. a) la estudiante

b) el consejero
b) el consejero
b) el consejero

B. *¿Es una pregunta?* You will hear a series of statements or questions. Listen carefully and circle the appropriate letter. Pay close attention to intonation.

1. a) statement
2. a) statement

b) question
b) question

3. a) statement   b) question
4. a) statement   b) question
5. a) statement   b) question

C. *Entrevista con la profesora Villegas.* Interview Professor Villegas for your school newspaper, using the following cues. Use the **Ud.** form of the verbs. Use the subject pronoun **Ud.** in your first question only. Professor Villegas will answer your questions.

    MODELO: (enseñar / inglés) → *¿Enseña Ud. inglés?* (No, enseño español.)

1. enseñar / cuatro clases   4. hablar / ruso
2. enseñar / italiano   5. gustar / la universidad
3. trabajar / por la noche

Un poco de todo

A. *Definiciones.* You will hear a series of statements. Each will be said twice. Write the number of the statement next to the word that is best defined by that statement.

___ una profesora   ___ un secretario

___ los clientes   ___ el chino

___ una biblioteca   ___ los estudiantes

B. *Listening Passage.* You will hear a brief passage about education in Hispanic countries. Then you will hear a series of statements about the passage. Circle *C* if the statement is true (*cierto*) or *F* if it is false (*falso*).

1. C F   2. C F   3. C F   4. C F

C. *Descripción.* Using the verbs you will hear, describe the actions in the drawing. You will hear a possible answer on the tape.

1. ...   2. ...   3. ...   4. ...   5. ...

D. *Y para terminar... Entrevista.* You will hear a series of questions about your studies. Each will be said twice. Answer based on your own experience. You will hear a possible answer on the tape. (If you prefer, stop the tape and write the answer.)

1. _____

2. _____

3. _____

4. _____

5. _____

Un paso más: Situaciones

En la biblioteca: Estudiando con un amigo

You will hear a brief conversation, partially printed in your manual, about studying. Then you will participate in a similar conversation. Complete it based on the cues suggested. You will hear the correct answer on the tape. (If you prefer, stop the tape and write the answer.)

—Oye, ¿ _____ ?

—A las tres y media. ¿Qué hora es?

—_____

—Hay tiempo todavía. ¿No quieres estudiar diez minutos más?

—Está bien. Entonces, ¿qué tal si _____ antes de tu clase?

—¡De acuerdo!

Here are the cues for your conversation:

clase de computación
2:45
pasar por la librería

CAPÍTULO

3

Vocabulario: Adjetivos

A. *¿Cuál es?* You will hear a series of descriptions. Each will be said twice. Circle the letter of the item or person described.

1. a)    b)

2. a)    b)

3. a)    b)

4. a)    b)

5. a)    b)

B. *Descripciones: ¿Cómo son?* Describe the following fathers and their sons by using one adjective from each of the following pairs to answer the questions you will hear. You will hear a possible answer on the tape. First, listen to the adjectives.

alto / bajo   rubio / moreno
delgado / gordo   joven / viejo

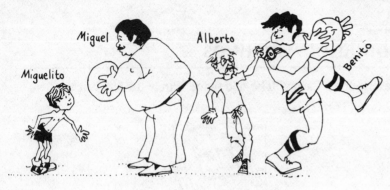

MODELO: Miguel es _____ , _____ , _____ y _____ .

1. ...   2. ...   3. ...   4. ...

Pronunciación y ortografía: *d*

A. Spanish *d* has two pronunciations. At the beginning of a phrase or sentence and after *n* or *l*, it is pronounced similar to English *d* as in dog. In all other cases, it is pronounced like the English sound *th* in ano*th*er. Repeat the following words and phrases, imitating the speaker. The type of *d* you should be using is indicated at the beginning of each line.

1. [d] diez dos docena doctor ¿dónde? el doctor el dinero grande
2. [đ] mucho dinero adiós usted casado ¿adónde? la doctora gordo todo

B. Repeat the following sentences, imitating the speaker.

1. ¿Dónde está el dinero?
2. David Dávila es doctor.
3. Dos y diez son doce.
4. ¿Qué estudia usted?
5. Delia es delgada, ¿verdad? (*right?*)

C. It is very common in the rapid speech of some Hispanic countries or regions to drop the [đ] sound when it appears between two vowels or at the end of a word. Thus, **Jurado** will sound like **Jurao**, and **¿verdad?** will sound like **¿verdá?** Listen to these words.

1. universidad libertad amistad (*friendship*)
2. lavado (*washed*) limpiado (*clean/cleaned*) casado comprometido (*engaged*)

D. You will hear a series of words containing the letter *d*. Each will be said twice. Circle the letter of the *d* sound you hear.

1. a) d   b. đ   4. a) d   b) đ
2. a) d   b) đ   5. a) d   b) đ
3. a) d   b) đ   6. a) d   b) đ

Estructuras

5. Expressing *to be*: Present Tense of **ser**; Summary of Uses

A. *Minidiálogo: En la oficina de la profesora Castro.* You will hear a dialogue followed by two statements about the dialogue. Circle the number of the statement that best summarizes the dialogue. In this exercise, you will practice listening for the main idea.

1   2

B. *¿Quiénes son?* Practice identifying people, using the oral cues.

MODELO: José (mecánico) → <u>José es mecánico</u>.

1. Mariluz
2. el señor Barrios
3. tú

4. Tomás y Ernesto
5. Araceli y yo

C. *¿De dónde son?* Practice telling where people are from, using the oral cues.

MODELO: (María / Colombia) → <u>María es de Colombia</u>.

1. ...   2. ...   3. ...   4. ...   5. ...

D. *¿Para quién son los regalos?* You need to give gifts to several of your relatives and friends, and money is no object! Select appropriate gifts for them from the following list. First, listen to the list.

la calculadora
los libros de filosofía
la camioneta

las novelas románticas
los discos (*records*) de Madonna

Use the phrases **por eso, para ella,** and **para él,** as in the model.

MODELO: (Su [*Your*] hermano Juan es estudiante universitario.) →
          <u>Por eso los libros de filosofía son para él.</u>

1. ...   2. ...   3. ...   4. ...

E. *Descripción.* You will hear a series of questions. Each will be said twice. Answer based on the corresponding drawing.

1.

2.

3.

4.

Vocabulario: Los números 31–100

A. *Dictado: El inventario.* You and a friend, Elisabet, are taking inventory at the university bookstore where you work. Write out the numerals as she dictates the list to you. She will say each number twice. ¡OJO! Items are given in random order. First, listen to the list of words.

_____ mochilas   _____ novelas

_____ lápices   _____ calculadoras

_____ cuadernos   _____ libros de texto

B. *En el periódico.* The following list of phone numbers is taken from a Hispanic newspaper. You will hear a series of questions about the numbers. Each will be said twice. Answer based on the list. First, look at the list. Don't be distracted by unfamiliar vocabulary.

EDITORA PASO DEL NORTE
FUNDADA EL DIA 17 DE FEBRERO DE 1976

DIARIO DE JUAREZ

OFICINAS Y TALLERES
Ave. Paseo Triunfo de la República y Anillo
Envolvente del Pronaf. Cd. Juárez, Chih. Mex.

PRESIDENTE Y DIRECTOR GENERAL
Osvaldo Rodríguez Borunda

JEFE DE REDACCION
Jesús Luis Ceniceros
Cervantes
JEFE DE INFORMACION
Roberto Abrego Salazar
SOCIALES
Esmeralda Torres B.

GERENTE DE PUBLICIDAD
Jorge Castro Obregón

DEPORTES
Ramón Guzmán Gallegos
RELACIONES PUBLICAS
Jaime Martínez O.

TELEFONOS

Dirección General	13-08-16
Gerencia General	13-09-55
Jefatura de Redacción	13-28-64, 16-43-83
Jefatura de Información	13-28-64, 16-35-85
Información General	16-35-85, 13-28-64
Sociales y Deportes	13-82-87
Publicidad	13-02-44, 13-18-72
Clasificado	16-09-09, 16-03-76
Clasificado	16-09-66, 16-00-50
Administrador/Compras	16-16-85
Admón. Crédito y Cobranzas	13-28-86
Recepción/Suscripciones	16-00-06

REPRESENTANTES EN MEXICO
"LEMUS" Representaciones Periodísticas Tel. 286-02-02
OFICINAS EN CHIHUAHUA
Ave. Universidad No. 1502 Tel. 13-44-03, 13-45-85, 13-41-81
EN NUEVO CASAS GRANDES
5 de Mayo No. 400 y Alvaro Obregón Tel. 4-25-25
EL PASO, TEXAS.
10737 Gateway West Suite 108 Ph. (915) 595-07-32 595-07-42
SERVICIOS INFORMATIVOS
UPI, EXCELSIOR, REUTER y LEMUS
Precio del Ejemplar $400.00 Domingos $300.00
Atrasados el Doble

MODELO: (¿Cuál es el teléfono de la Gerencia [*Management*] General?) →
Es el <u>trece - cero nueve - cincuenta y cinco</u>.

1. ...   2. ...   3. ...   4. ...

Estructuras

6. Describing: Adjectives; Gender, Number, and Position

A. *Descripciones.* You will hear four incomplete sentences followed by a series of adjectives. Each sentence will be said twice. Listen carefully and circle the adjective or adjectives that could be used to describe the person or persons mentioned in each sentence. Then repeat the completed sentence.

MODELO: (La señora Vásquez es...) alto rubia simpática →
La señora Vázquez es <u>rubia y simpática.</u>

1. (...)   amables   inteligente   bonita
2. (...)   paciente   bajos   gordo
3. (...)   joven   romántica   optimista
4. (...)   casados   perezosa   solteras

B. *¿Cómo son?* Practice describing family members and friends, using the oral and written cues. Make any of the sentences negative or change any of the adjectives given, as needed. Use **mi** (*my*) with singular nouns and **mis** (*my*) with plural ones, as in the cues. Feel free to substitute real names as needed.

MODELO: mi familia (rico) → Mi familia no es rica.

1. mi padre
2. mi madre
3. mi amigo Luis
4. mis amigas Teresa y Graciela
5. mi familia

C. *¿De dónde son y qué idioma hablan?* Your friend Carmen is asking you about some of the exchange students on campus. You will hear each of her questions twice. Answer according to the model, giving the nationality of the persons she mentions and the language they might speak.

MODELO: (¿Evaristo es de Portugal?) → <u>Sí, es portugués y habla portugués</u>.

1. ...   2. ...   3. ...   4. ...   5. ...

D. *¿Qué dicen* (are saying) *estas personas?* Use the Spanish equivalents of *this* and *these* and the correct form of an adjective from the following list to tell what these people might be saying. For example, the man in the first drawing might be saying the Spanish equivalent of "This book is large." You will hear a possible answer on the tape. First, listen to the list of adjectives.

moreno   grande   corto   pequeño   alto

1.

2.

3.

4.

5.

E. *Entrevista: Opiniones.* You will hear a series of questions. Each will be said twice. Answer according to your experience. No answers will be given on the tape. (If you prefer, stop the tape and write the answer.)

1. _____

2. _____

3. _____

4. _____

5. _____

Un poco de todo

A. *Conversación: Hablando de fotos.* You will hear a conversation between two roommates, printed in your manual, about the brother of one of them. Then you will participate in a similar conversation about a sister. Make any necessary changes in the dialogue. You will hear the correct answer on the tape.

—¿Quién es el joven alto y moreno en esta foto?
—Es mi hermano Julio.
—¡Qué guapo es!
—¿Te gustaría conocerlo? (*Would you like to meet him?*)
—¡Sí! ¡Claro que sí! (*Of course!*)

B. *Estrategias: Recognizing Cognate Patterns.* As you know, cognates are words that are similar in meaning and form in two languages. Knowing about cognate patterns will help you recognize more Spanish cognates of English.

One common pattern involves word endings or suffixes. Note how the following Spanish suffixes correspond to English suffixes. In some cases, the suffix itself is a cognate. In others, the stem to which the suffix is added is the cognate.

universi*dad*	=	universi*ty*
ac*ción*	=	ac*tion*
mansi*ón*	=	mans*ion*
poé*tico*/poé*tica*	=	poet*ic*
polí*tico*/polí*tica*	=	polit*ical*
constante*mente*	=	constant*ly*
estudi*oso*/estudi*osa*	=	studi*ous*

You will hear a series of words. Listen carefully to them, paying particular attention to suffixes, and circle the letter of the English equivalent.

1. a) attraction   b) attractive
2. a) technically   b) technical
3. a) fury   b) furious
4. a) finally   b) finalist
5. a) liberate   b) liberty

C. *¿Cómo son?* In the preceding exercise, you practiced listening for suffixes. In this exercise, you will use prefixes to form the opposite of the adjectives given. First, listen to the list, paying close attention to the indicated prefixes.

*ir*racional   *in*justo   *des*agradable   *im*paciente   *anti*comunista
*ir*responsable   *in*competente   *des*leal   *im*práctico   *anti*patriótico

Now, answer negatively the questions you will hear, using words chosen from the preceding list.

MODELO: (Él es competente, ¿verdad?) No, al contrario. Es incompetente.

1. ...   2. ...   3. ...   4. ...

D. *Y para terminar... Preguntas.* In this exercise, you will practice asking a friend information about herself. Form questions based on the written cues and repeat the question you hear. You will hear an answer to your questions on the tape. (If you prefer, stop the tape and write the question.)

MODELO: nombre → ¿Cómo te llamas? (Me llamo Silvia Hurtado.)

1. lugar de origen: _____

2. personalidad: _____

3. trabajar: _____

4. estudiar: _____

CAPÍTULO

4

Vocabulario: La familia y los parientes

A. *La familia Muñoz*. You will hear a series of statements about the Muñoz family. Each will be said twice. Circle *C* if the statement is true (*cierto*) or *F* if it is false (*falso*). First, look at the family tree.

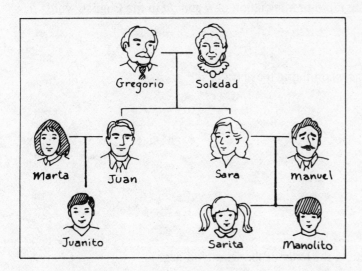

1. C F   2. C F   3. C F   4. C F   5. C F

B. *Definiciones*. You will hear a series of definitions of family relationships. Each will be said twice. Listen carefully and write the number of the definition next to the word defined. First, listen to the list of words.

____ mi abuelo   ____ mi prima

____ mi tía   ____ mi tío

____ mi hermano   ____ mi abuela

C. *Conversación. Hablando de la familia*. You will hear a conversation, partially printed in your manual, about the number of people in a family. Then you will participate in a similar conversation. Complete it based on the cues suggested and using **tengo** to express *I have*. You will hear the correct answer on the tape.

A: —Tienes una familia muy grande ¿Cuántos son?

B: —Bueno, _____.

A: —¿Y cuántos primos?

B: —¡Uf! _____ un montón. Más de _____.

Here are the cues for your conversation:

4 hermanos, 1 hermana
16

Pronunciación y ortografía: *r* and *rr*

A. The letter *r* has two pronunciations in Spanish: the trilled *r* (written as *rr* between vowels or as *r* at the beginning of a word), and the flap *r*, which appears in all other positions. Because mispronunciations can alter the meaning of a word, it is important to distinguish between these two pronunciations of the Spanish *r*. For example: **coro** (*chorus*) and **corro** (*I run*).

The flap *r* is similar to the sound produced by the rapid pronunciation of *tt* and *dd* in the English words Betty and ladder.

petty / pero   *sadder* / Sara   *motor* / moro

Repeat the following words, phrases, and sentences, imitating the speaker.

1. arte   gracias   pero   hablar   triste
2. ruso   Roberto   real   reportero   rebelde
3. burro   corral   carro   barra   corro
4. el nombre correcto   el precio del cuaderno
   las residencias   una mujer refinada
   rosas grandes   Puerto Rico
5. Este error es raro.
   Soy el primo de Roque Ramírez.
   Enrique, Carlos y Rosita regresan mañana.

B. *¿R o rr?* You will hear a series of words. Circle the letter of the word you hear.

1. a) ahora   b) ahorra   4. a) coral   b) corral
2. a) caro   b) carro   5. a) pero   b) perro
3. a) coro   b) corro

C. *Trabalenguas.* You will hear the following Spanish tongue twister. Listen to it once; then repeat it, imitating the speaker.

R con R guitarra.   Mira qué rápido corren (*run*)
R con R barril.   los carros del ferrocarril (*railroad*).

Estructuras

7.   Expressing Actions: Present Tense of *-er* and *-ir* Verbs; More About Subject Pronouns

A. *Minidiálogo: Por la tarde, en casa de la familia Robles.* You will hear a dialogue followed by a series of statements. Circle the letter of the name of the person who might have made each statement. In this exercise, you will practice listening for general as well as specific information.

1. a) el señor Robles   b) la hija
2. a) el señor Robles   b) la hija
3. a) el señor Robles   b) la hija
4. a) el señor Robles   b) la hija

B. *En clase.* Practice telling about what happens in class, using the subjects you hear and the written cues. ¡OJO! Remember that subject pronouns are not always used in Spanish.

MODELO: escribir los ejercicios (unos estudiantes) → <u>Unos estudiantes escriben los ejercicios.</u>

1. leer el libro de texto
2. comprender bien la lección
3. abrir mi mochila
4. insistir en hablar en español
5. deber escuchar (*to listen*) al profesor
6. aprender mucho

C. *¿Qué hacen?* (What are they doing?) Tell what the people in the drawings are doing when you hear the corresponding number. You will hear a possible answer on the tape.

1.

2.

3.

4.

1. ...   2. ...   3. ...   4. ...

D. *Entrevista.* You will hear a series of questions. Each will be said twice. Answer based on your own experience. No answers will be given on the tape. (If you prefer, stop the tape and write the answer.)

1. _____
2. _____
3. _____
4. _____
5. _____

Vocabulario: Las relaciones sentimentales

Definiciones. You will hear a series of statements. Each will be said twice. Circle the letter of the word that is best defined by each statement.

1. a) la luna de miel   b) la amistad
2. a) la boda   b) el divorcio
3. a) cariñoso   b) el novio
4. a) la cita   b) el amor
5. a) el noviazgo   b) el divorcio
6. a) la iglesia   b) la luna de miel

Estructuras

8. Pointing Out People and Things: Demonstrative Adjectives

A. *Minidiálogo: Delante de una iglesia.* You will hear a dialogue, between a father and his son, followed by a series of statements. Circle the letter of the person who might have made each statement.

1. a) el padre   b) Panchito
2. a) el padre   b) Panchito
3. a) el padre   b) Panchito
4. a) el padre   b) Panchito

B. *El día de la boda.* Describe the people and things you see at your friend's wedding. Use the appropriate form of the demonstrative adjective you hear and the written cues.

MODELO: señora / la madre de la novia (ese) → <u>Esa señora es La madre de la novia.</u>

1. iglesia / grande
2. señoritas / hermanas del novio
3. joven / amigo de la novia
4. regalos (*presents*) / bonito
5. niños / sobrinos del novio

C. *Recuerdos de su luna de miel en México.* Your friends want to know all about your trip to Mexico. Answer their questions, using an appropriate form of the demonstrative adjective **aquel** and the oral cues.

MODELO: ¿Qué tal el restaurante El Charro? (excelente) → ¡Aquel restuarante es excelente!

1. ¿Qué tal el hotel Libertad?

2. ¿Y los dependientes del hotel?

3. ¿Qué tal la ropa (*clothing*) en el Mercado de la Merced?

4. ¿Y los periódicos de la capital?

D. *Dictado: El día de la boda.* You will hear five sentences. Each will be said twice. Write the missing words.

1. _____ señora es la madre del novio y _____ señor es su (*his*) padre.

2. _____ regalos (*presents*) son para los novios.

3. _____ señorita es la hermana de la novia y _____ mujer es su prima.

4. ¿Y qué es _____ ? Es el champán para la recepción.

Un poco de todo

A. *En el periódico: Sociales.* You will hear an excerpt from an article printed in the society section of an Hispanic newspaper. Then you will hear two statements about the article. Circle the number of the statement that best summarizes the article. In this exercise you will practice getting the main idea, so don't be distracted by unfamiliar vocabulary.

1 2

B. *Dictado: Detalles de la boda.* Now rewind the tape and listen to the article again. Listen carefully and write down the requested information from the article. First, listen to the information that is requested.

La hora de la boda: _____

Los nombres de los esposos: _____ y _____

¿Hubo (*Was there*) recepción después de la boda? _____

C. *Listening Passage.* You will hear a brief passage about important members of some Hispanic families, **los suegros** (in-laws). Then you will hear a series of statements about the passage. Circle C if the statement is true (*cierto*) or F if it is false (*falso*).

The following words and phrases will appear in the listening passage. Listen to them before the passage is read.

encontrar *to find*
ayudan (*they*) *help*
sus gastos *their expenses*

el resultado *result*
juntos *together*

1. C F   2. C F   3. C F   4. C F

D. *Y para terminar... Descripción: Una reunión familiar.* You will hear a series of questions. Each will be said twice. Answer each question based on the drawing. You will hear a possible answer on the tape.

1. ...   2. ...   3. ...   4. ...   5. ...   6. ...   7. ...   8. ...

Un paso más: Situaciones

Presentaciones

In the following conversations, you will practice handling introductions in Spanish, in informal as well as formal situations. Read the conversations silently, along with the speaker.

En casa...

—Abuelo, quiero presentarle a Adolfo... Adolfo Álvarez Montes. Somos compañeros de clase en la universidad.
—Encantado, don Antonio.
—Igualmente, Adolfo. Bienvenido a nuestra casa.

En clase...

—Profesora Benítez, quisiera presentarle a Laura Sánchez Trujillo. Es mi amiga salvadoreña.
—Mucho gusto, Laura.
—El gusto es mío, profesora.

En la cafetería...

—Quico, te presento a Adela. Es amiga de Julio, ¿sabes?
—Mucho gusto, Adela.
—Igualmente.
—¿Qué tal si tomamos un café?
—¡De acuerdo!

Now you will participate in two conversations, one in which you are introduced to the father of one of your friends, and one in which you introduce two of your friends to each other. Choose your responses from the list below. No answer will be given on the tape. First, listen to the list.

quisiera (quiero) presentarle a...   mucho gusto
te presento a...

Here is the first conversation. Your friend will introduce you to her father. Your name is Kim.

—Papá, le presento a Kim. Somos compañeras en la clase de español.

—_____

—El gusto es mío, Kim.

Here is the second conversation. Begin by introducing your friend Luis to another friend, Julia.

—Julia, _____
—Mucho gusto, Luis.
—Encantado.

REPASO

A. *Conversaciones privadas.* You will overhear a conversation in which two people talk about some of their acquaintances. Then you will hear two sentences in English about the conversation. Circle the number of the statement that best describes the conversation. Try to get the gist of the conversation, and don't worry about unfamiliar vocabulary.

1   2

B. *¿Dónde están estas personas?* (Where are these people?) You will hear five brief conversations or parts of conversations. Listen carefully and write the location in which each conversation is taking place next to the number of the conversation. First, listen to the list of possible locations.

una casa   una clase de matemáticas
una biblioteca   una librería
una clase de lenguas   una fiesta estudiantil

1. _____   4. _____

2. _____   5. _____

3. _____

C. *Estrategias: Repaso.* In previous **Estrategias** sections, you have practiced recognizing cognates and cognate patterns as well as guessing the meaning of words from context. In Exercises C and D you will review some of those listening and reading strategies by working with the following list of courses offered by a learning institution in Venezuela.

What would you expect to see in a list of courses? the names of specific courses? a brief description of them? the days and times the classes meet? the names of the professors? If you answered yes to each of these questions, you are correct. Take a few seconds to scan the ad, trying to find the major blocks of information in it. Pay no attention to typographical errors! Many ads in all languages have them.

You will hear a series of cognates from the chart, in a brief context. The arrows to the right of the ad indicate where you will find the cognates. Listen carefully, paying particular attention to the endings and answering these questions as you go along.

UNIVERSIDAD PEDAGOGICA
EXPERIMENTAL LIBERTADOR

INSTITUTO PEDAGOGICO
"J. M. SISO MARTINEZ"

CURSOS DE EXTENSION

El Consejo Directivo del Instituto Pedagógico "J.M. Siso Martínez", a través de la Subdirección de Extensión, ofrece los siguientes cursos de mejoramiento y actualización profesional:

DENOMINACION	DIRIGIDO A	DURACION, DIA Y HORA	INICIO Y CULMINACION	FACILITADOR
Expresión Oral	Docentes, locutores, oradores, comunicadores e interesados	24 horas Lunes 2:00 a 5:00 p.m.	19-03-90 al 21-05-90	Lic. Magaly Hurtado
Uso y Aplicación del Osciloscopio	Docentes de Física y Electricidad que trabajen con corriente alterna, estudiantes de las especialidades relacionadas a electricidad	21 horas Martes 8:00 a 11:00 am.	20-03-90 al 15-05-90	Prof. Edgar Carrillo
Auxiliar de Biblioteca	Interesados en adquirir conocimientos, habilidades y destrezas en el manejo bibliotecario	20 horas Miércoles 8:00 a.m. a 12:00 m.	21-03-90 al 25-04-90	Lic. Leida de Azuaje
Primeros Auxilios	A todos los interesados en adquirir conocimientos para la aplicación de los primeros auxilios	21 horas Miércoles 8:00 a.m. a 12:00 m.	21-03-90 al 09-05-90	Dr. Erick Moreira

1. **Extensión** probably means
   a. extended
   b. extension
2. **Duración**, refers to
   a. duration
   b. durability
3. **Aplicación** refers to
   a. an applicant
   b. an application
4. The word **electricidad** means
   a. electric
   b. electricity
5. **Habilidades** means
   a. abilities
   b. able

Now you will hear a brief passage adapted from the list of courses. Try to guess the meaning of the following words from the context of the passage. First, listen to the words.

adquirir   conocimientos   bibliotecario

1. The word **adquirir** is
   a. an adjective
   b. a noun
   c. a verb
2. **Adquirir** probably means
   a. to adhere
   b. to acquire
   c. to advertise
3. In the phrase **adquirir conocimientos, conocimeintos** probably means
   a. knowledge
   b. consignments
   c. comments
4. The **bibliotecario** most likely describes someone who
   a. writes bibliographies
   b. works in a bookstore
   c. works in a library

D. *Preguntas.* Stop the tape and take another look at the list of courses from Venezuela. At this point you should be able to understand much more of it than you did the first time you scanned it. Then start the tape and answer the questions you hear based on information in the chart. You will hear each question only once.

1. ...   2. ...   3. ...   4. ...   5. ...

E. *Conversación: En la facultad.* You will hear a conversation, partially printed in your manual, between two friends who pass each other on campus. Then you will participate in a similar conversation, playing Luisa's role. Answer based on your own experience. No answers will be given on the tape.

ALFREDO: Hola, Luisa. ¿Qué tal?

LUISA: _____

ALFREDO: Así así. ¿Cuándo es el examen en la clase de geografía?

LUISA: _____

ALFREDO: Buena suerte (*luck*), ¿eh? ¿Trabajas en la librería hoy?

LUISA: _____

ALFREDO: Bueno, hasta luego, Luisa.

LUISA: _____

F. *Descripción: ¿Una familia típica?* You will hear a series of questions about the following cartoon. Each will be said twice. Answer based on your interpretation of the drawing. You will hear a possible answer on tape. First, take time to look at the cartoon and listen to the list of adjectives you may need to answer some of the questions.

SÓLO PAPÁ

bueno   paciente   serio   simpático   malo   cariñoso

1. ...   2. ...   3. ...   4. ...   5. ...   6. ...   7. ...   8. Mi...

G. *Un día típico.* Practice talking about your routine and that of others, using the written cues. When you hear the corresponding number, form sentences using the words given in the order given, making any necessary changes and additions. You will hear a possible answer on the tape.

1. (yo) llegar / universidad / temprano / 7:30 A.M.
2. profesores / llegar / temprano / también
3. (yo) tener / clase de computación / 11:00 A.M.
4. ese / clase / ser / difícil (*difficult*) / pero / ser / muy / interesante
5. (yo) comer / en / cafetería / 12:30 P.M.

6. con frecuencia, / mis amigos y yo / estudiar / en / biblioteca
7. (yo) regresar / casa / 6:15 P.M.
8. ahora / (yo) vivir / casa / pequeño / con mi padres
9. el próximo (next) año / (yo) querer / vivir / en / residencia

H. *Entrevista.* You will hear a series of questions about yourself. Each will be said twice. Answer based on your own experience. No answers will be given on the tape. (If you prefer, stop the tape and write the answer.)

1. _____
2. _____
3. _____
4. _____
5. _____
6. _____
7. _____
8. _____
9. _____
10. _____

CAPÍTULO

5

Vocabulario: La ropa; ¿De qué color es?

A. *Definiciones.* You will hear a series of statements. Each will be said twice. Circle the letter of the phrase defined by each. In this exercise, you will practice listening for the main idea of the sentence. Try not to be distracted by unfamiliar vocabulary.

1. a) grises   b) azules
2. a) pantalones cortos b) una bolsa
3. a) la corbata   b) la cartera
4. a) verde   b) rojo
5. a) la mochila   b) el abrigo
6. a) el cinturón   b) el algodón
7. a) rosado   b) la seda
8. a) de cuadros   b) un par

B. *Identificaciones.* Identify the items after you hear the corresponding number. Begin each sentence with **Es un...**, **Es una...**, or **Son...** .

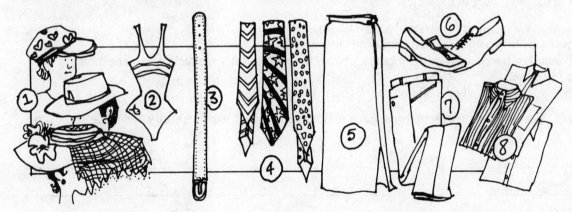

C. *¿Qué ropa llevan estas personas?* You will hear a series of questions. Answer based on the drawings. You will be describing the clothing these people are wearing and telling who they might be or where they might be. You will hear a possible answer on the tape.

1. ... ...   2. ... ...   3. ... ... Están...

Pronunciación y ortografía: *b/v*

A. Spanish *b* and *v* are pronounced exactly the same way. At the beginning of a phrase, or after *m* or *n*, *b* and *v* are pronounced like the English *b*, as a stop; that is, no air is allowed to escape through the lips. In all other positions, *b* and *v* are fricatives; that is, they are produced by allowing some air to escape through the lips. There is no equivalent for this sound in English.

Repeat the following words and phrases, imitating the speaker. Note that the type of *b* sound you will hear is marked at the beginning of the series.

1. [b] bueno   viejo   verde   barato   boda   hombre
2. [ƀ] llevar   libro   pobre   abrigo   universidad   abuelo
3. [b/ƀ] bueno / es bueno   busca / Ud. busca   bien / muy bien   en Venezuela / de Venezuela   vende / se vende
4. [b/ƀ] beber   bebida   vivir   biblioteca   Babel   vívido

B. *Dictado.* You will hear four sentences. Each will be said twice. Listen carefully and write what you hear.

1. _____
2. _____
3. _____
4. _____

Estructuras

9. Expressing Actions and States: *Tener, venir, preferir, querer*, and *poder*; Some idioms with *tener*

A. *No es por falta de ganas* (desire)... In the following dialogue two friends will discuss their plans for the evening. Listen to the dialogue; then choose the statement that best summarizes it. In this exercise, you will practice listening for general information. Don't be distracted by unfamiliar vocabulary. Use the drawing to establish a context for the listening practice.

1   2

B. *Es la semana de exámenes.* Practice telling about what you and your friends do during exam week. ¡OJO! Remember that subject pronouns are not always used in Spanish.

1. tener muchos exámenes
2. venir a la biblioteca
3. leer cien páginas en dos horas
4. ¡ya no (*no longer*) poder leer más!
5. preferir estudiar en la cafetería
6. regresar a la residencia a las diez y media

C. *Gustos y preferencias.* Ask a friend about her clothing preferences during a shopping trip. Form questions based on the written cues and using tag questions. Repeat the answer that you hear on the tape. Then, when you hear your friend's answer, ask for more information. Follow the model.

MODELO: preferir / los zapatos azules →
—<u>Prefieres los zapatos azules, ¿no?</u>
(—Bueno... En realidad prefiero los verdes.)
—<u>¿Por qué prefieres los verdes?</u>
(—Porque el verde es mi color favorito.)

1. preferir / las faldas rojas
2. querer / comprar / los pantalones verdes
3. me gusta / mucho ropa de lana

D. *¿Qué hacemos* (are we doing) *esta noche?* You and your friends are talking about what has to be done and what you would like to do tonight. You will hear each question twice. Answer, using the written cues.

1. Sí,...
2. mirar la televisión
3. Sí,...
4. estar en la cafetería con Tomás
5. Sí,...
6. bailar hasta (*until*) muy tarde

Vocabulario: ¿Cómo estás? ¿Dónde estás?

A. *¿Cómo están hoy?* Tell how each person mentioned on the tape is feeling today, using the written cues.

MODELO: bien (Ud.) → <u>Ud. está bien.</u>

1. bien
2. así así
3. enfermo
4. enfermas también
5. muy bien, ¿verdad?

B. *Preguntas.* You will hear a series of questions about you and your friends. Each will be said twice. Answer based on your own experience. You will hear a possible answer on the tape. (If you prefer, stop the tape and write the answer.)

1. _____

2. _____

3. _____

4. _____

5. _____

Estructuras

10. *¿Ser o estar?*: Summary of Uses of *ser* and *estar*

A. *Minidiálogo: Una conversación telefónica entre una esposa que está en un viaje de negocios y su esposo que está en casa.* You will hear half of a phone conversation followed by a series of statements about the conversation. Circle the letter of the person who might have made each statement. In this exercise, you will practice listening for specific information. Don't be distracted by unfamiliar vocabulary.

1. a) el esposo   b) la esposa
2. a) el esposo   b) la esposa
3. a) el esposo   b) la esposa
4. a) el esposo   b) la esposa

B. *Marcos, ¿qué tal?* Tell how your friend Marcos seems to be feeling on these different occasions, using one of these adjectives. First, listen to the list of adjectives.

nervioso furioso triste contento preocupado

1.  2.  3.  4.  5.

1. ...   2. ...   3. ...   4. ...   5. ...

C. *¿Quiénes son?* Tell who the young people in this family photograph are, using the oral cues.

1. ...   2. ...   3. ...   4. ...   5. ...   6. ...

D. *¿Ser o estar?* Susana is not sure she has understood what you said. Answer her questions in the affirmative, using **ser** or **estar**, as appropriate.

MODELO: (¿Tú? ¿Muy bien hoy?) → Sí, ¡estoy muy bien hoy!

1. ...   2. ...   3. ...   4. ...   5. ...   6. ...

Un poco de todo

A. *Estrategias: Listening for the Main Parts of a Sentence.* In Chapter 1, before you had learned anything at all about Spanish verbs, you practiced identifying verbs in sentences and guessing their meaning from context. Since then, you have learned a lot about the verb system in Spanish, as well as about agreement and word order.

In the following exercise, you will continue to practice identifying parts of sentences. This time, however, you will not see the sentences. Rewind the tape and listen again if you need to.

You will hear three sentences, followed by two questions about each. Circle the letter of the correct answer. ¡OJO! There may be more than one.

1. a) a verb   b) a subject   c) an adjective
2. a) ellos   b) Uds.   c) nosotros
3. a) el impermeable   b) el hombre   c) Leonor
4. a) el impermeable   b) el hombre   c) Leonor
5. a) yo (*speaker*)   b) los perros   c) las sobrinas
6. a) yo (*speaker*)   b) las primas   c) las sobrinas

B. *En busca de regalos para papá.* You will hear a conversation between a brother and sister, who need to buy a birthday gift for their father. Do not be distracted by unfamiliar vocabulary. As you listen, circle the items that they decide to purchase.

C. *Nuestra vida como estudiantes.* You will hear a series of questions. Each will be said twice. Answer based on your own experience. You will hear a possible answer on the tape. (If you prefer, stop the tape and write your answer.)

1. _____

2. _____

3. _____

4. _____

5. _____

D. *Y para terminar... Descripción: Escenas sentimentales.* Describe the following drawings by answering the corresponding questions. You will hear a possible answer on the tape. First, take time to look at each drawing.

1.

a. ...   b. ...   c. ...   d. ...   e. ...

2.

a. ...   b. ...   c. ...   d. ...   e. ...

CAPÍTULO

6

Vocabulario: ¿Dónde venden... ?

A. *Descripción*. You will hear a series of descriptions. Listen carefully and write the number of the description next to the location or scene described. Try to get the gist of the descriptions and don't be distracted by unfamiliar vocabulary.

a) ___

c) ___

b) ___

d) ___

B. *Preguntas*. Verify information about stores and shopping customs in the Hispanic world by asking a Mexican friend questions based on these cues. Use tag questions. After you repeat the question you hear, you will hear a possible answer on the tape.

MODELO: no hay / mercados / en / ciudades grandes →
<u>No hay mercados en las ciudades grandes, ¿verdad?</u>
¡Claro que sí! Hay muchos mercados en la Ciudad de México, por ejemplo.

1. no regatear (tú) / en / almacén
2. vender (ellos) de todo / en / centros comerciales
3. no hay / rebajas / en / supermercados
4. pagar (tú) / precios fijos / en / mercado

Pronunciación y ortografía: *c, qu*

A. The [k] sound in Spanish can be written two ways: before the vowels *a, o,* and *u* it is written as *c*; before *i* and *e*, it is written as *qu*. The letter *k* itself appears only in words that are borrowed from other languages. Unlike the English [k] sound, the Spanish sound is not aspirated; that is, no air is allowed to escape when it is pronounced. Compare the following pairs of English words in which the first [k] sound is aspirated and the second is not.

can / scan   cold / scold   kit / skit

Repeat the following words, imitating the speaker. Remember to pronounce the [k] sound without aspiration.

1. casa cosa rico roca comida mercado corbatas
2. ¿quién? Quito aquí ¿qué? pequeño porque paquete quiero
3. kilo kilogramo kiosco kerosén kilómetro karate

B. *Dictado.* You will hear a series of words. Each will be said twice. Listen carefully and write what you hear.

1. _____   4. _____

2. _____   5. _____

3. _____   6. _____

Estructuras

11. Expressing Possession: Possessive Adjectives (Unstressed)

A. *Minidiálogo: En el periódico.* You will hear a letter to *Querida Antonia* and her response, followed by a series of statements. Circle the letter of the person or persons who might have made each statement. In this exercise, you will practice listening for specific and general information.

1. a) Sin Zapatos   b) Antonia   c) los padres de Sin Zapatos
2. a) Sin Zapatos   b) Antonia   c) los padres de Sin Zapatos
3. a) Sin Zapatos   b) Antonia   c) los padres de Sin Zapatos
4. a) Sin Zapatos   b) Antonia   c) los padres de Sin Zapatos

B. *¿Cómo es la tienda de Isabel?* Practice telling about Isabel's store, using the oral and written cues.

MODELO: (tienda) grande → <u>Su tienda es grande</u>.

1. simpático
2. fijo
3. caro

4. muy de moda (¡OJO! estar)
5. nuevo

C. *¡Qué confusión!* Sara asks you to clarify what belongs to whom. You will hear each of her questions twice. Answer according to the model.

MODELO: (¿Es la casa de Paco?) → <u>No, no es su casa</u>.

1. ...   2. ...   3. ...   4. ...   5. ...

D. *Entrevista.* You will hear a series of questions about your family and friends. Each will be said twice. Answer based on your own experience. No answers will be given on the tape. (If you prefer, stop the tape and write the answer.)

1. _____
2. _____
3. _____
4. _____
5. _____
6. _____

Vocabulario: ¿Qué día es hoy?

Dictado: El horario del profesor Velásquez. Imagine that you are Professor Velásquez' secretary and that you are filling in her weekly calendar. Listen carefully as she tells you her schedule for this week, and fill in the blanks in the calendar. Some of the entries have already been made. Rewind the tape and listen again if you need to.

lunes	martes	miércoles	jueves	viernes
mañana 10:45 AM: Clase de conversación	mañana _: dentista	mañana _:	mañana _:	mañana _:
tarde _:	tarde _:	tarde _:	tarde 3:00PM: Clase de español	tarde _:

Estructuras

12. Expressing Destination and Future Actions: *Ir; ir + a +* Infinitive

A. *Minidiálogo: Un regalo para la «mamá» ecuatoriana.* You will hear a dialogue followed by a series of statements about the dialogue. Circle *C* if the statement is true or *F* if it is false. In this exercise, you will practice listening for specific information. The dialogue takes place in Ecuador.

1. C F   2. C F   3. C F   4. C F

B. *¿Adónde vas?* You will hear a series of sentences about what you like to do or want to do. Using the words and phrases listed below, tell where you would go to do these activities, following the model. First, listen to the list of words.

universidad	discoteca La Rueda	Restaurante Gallego
Almacén Robles	biblioteca	
mercado	farmacia	

> MODELO: (Te gusta estudiar y aprender cosas.) →
> <u>Por eso voy a la universidad</u>.

1. ...   2. ...   3. ...   4. ...   5. ...

C. *Entrevista.* You will hear a series of questions about what you plan to do. Each will be said twice. Answer based on your own experience. You will hear a possible answer on the tape. (If you prefer, stop the tape and write the answer.)

1. _____

2. _____

3. _____

4. _____

5. _____

6. _____

Vocabulario: Los números 100 y más

Preguntas. You will hear a series of questions. Answer, using the written cues. ¡OJO! **Cuánto pagaste por...?** means *How much did you pay for . . . ?*

> MODELO: (¿Cuánto pagaste por la radio?) $40,00 → <u>Cuarenta dólares</u>.

1. $938,00
2. $159.000,00
3. 33.507
4. 2.432.824

Estructuras

13. Describing: Comparisons

A. *Tipos y estereotipos.* You will hear a brief description of the people in the following drawing. Then you will hear a series of statements about them. Circle *C* if the statement is true or *F* if it is false.

1. C F   2. C F   3. C F   4. C F

B. *Un desacuerdo.* You and your friend Lourdes don't agree about anything! React to her statements negatively, using the written cues.

> MODELO: La clase de inglés es menos importante que la clase de español. (tan) →
> ¡No! La clase de inglés es tan importante como la clase de español.

1. El matrimonio es menos importante que la amistad.
2. Mi perro es más cariñoso que tu gato.
3. Las faldas son tan prácticas como los pantalones.
4. Mi familia es tan grande como tu familia.

C. *Un acuerdo perfecto.* Rafael and Carmen always do and have the same things. Describe their relationship, using the oral cues.

> MODELO: (beber / café) → Rafael bebe tanto café como Carmen.

1. ...   2. ...   3. ...   4. ...

Un poco de todo

A. *Dictado: La venta anual.* You will hear an ad for merchandise from a department store. It will be read twice. Listen carefully and write down the requested information. First, listen to the list of new words and expressions that appear in the ad, and the list of information for which you will be listening.

el hogar (*the home*)
vengan a visitarnos (*come visit us*)

el nombre del almacén: _____

el precio de los zapatos para señora: _____

el precio de los trajes para caballero (*men*): _____

tres cosas para el hogar: _____

_____ , _____ ,

el precio del estéreo: _____

el precio del sofá: _____

B. *Listening Passage.* You will hear a brief passage about a special market in Madrid, Spain. Then you will hear a series of incomplete statements about the passage. Circle the letter of the phrase that best completes each sentence, based on the passage.

1. a) el Rastro   b) el Rostro
2. a) de todo   b) sólo ropa y comida
3. a) buenos precios   b) precios fijos
4. a) descansar   b) regatear
5. a) ir temprano   b) ir de compras

C. *Y para terminar... Descripción: De compras en el mercado.* You will hear a series of statements about the following drawing. Circle *C* if the statement is true or *F* if it is false. Answer based on the drawing.

1. C F   2. C F   3. C F   4. C F   5. C F

Un paso más: Situaciones

A. *En una tienda de ropa.* In the following conversation, you will learn about talking to a salesperson about the clothes you are interested in purchasing. Read the dialogue silently, along with the speakers.

—¿Le atienden? ¿Qué desea?
—Hola, buenas. Busco un pantalón de algodón de color oscuro para mí.
—¿Qué talla usa?
—La trece, por lo general.
—¿Qué le parece este pantalón negro?
—No está mal. Y ¿qué tal una blusa de seda también?
—Cómo no. En su talla tenemos blusas de seda en color beige, rojo y gris perla. Son perfectas para este pantalón.
—¿Dónde me los puedo probar?

—Allí están los probadores. Si necesita algo, mi nombre es Méndez.
—Gracias.

B. *En una zapatería.* Now you will participate in a similar conversation, partially printed in your manual, about buying a pair of shoes. Complete it with information that is true for you. You will hear a possible answer on the tape.

—Buenas tardes. ¿En qué puedo servirle?

—Muy buenas. Busco _____

—¿De qué color?

— _____

—Pues aquí tenemos de todo. _____

—El _____ , por lo general.

—Bueno, tome asiento (*be seated*) mientras le busco unos pares para probar.

CAPÍTULO

7

Vocabulario: ¿Qué tiempo hace hoy?

A. *¿Qué tiempo hace?* You will hear a series of weather conditions. Each will be said twice. Give the number of the drawing to which each corresponds; then repeat the description. First, look at the drawings.

1.

2.

3.

4.

5.

B. *En el periódico: Hablando del clima.* Look at the following chart of temperatures from a Spanish newspaper from October. Then answer the questions about the chart. You will hear a possible answer on the tape. First, listen to the list of symbols.

TEMPERATURAS		MÁX.	MÍN.
Ámsterdam	D	12	4
Atenas	D	22	15
Barcelona	D	21	14
Berlín	Q	8	6
Bonn	Q	14	2
Bruselas	D	12	2
Buenos Aires	Q	17	12
Cairo, El	D	26	18
Caracas	D	26	20
Copenhague	D	9	3
Dublín	Q	12	8
Estocolmo	f	7	6
Francfort	Q	11	4
Ginebra	Q	13	11
Hamburgo	Q	8	6
Lisboa	D	19	13
Londres	D	13	1
Madrid	A	20	10
México	Q	25	10
Miami	Q	27	23
Moscú	D	2	–6
Munich	f	8	7
Nueva York	D	19	9
Oslo	f	8	4
París	D	13	5
Rabat	Q	23	18
R. de Janeiro	P	25	20
Roma	D	23	15
Tokio	Q	17	12
Viena	Q	12	10
Zurich	Q	16	9

A = agradable
C = mucho calor
c = calor
D = despejado (*clear*)
F = mucho frío

f = frío
H = heladas (*frost*)
N = nevadas
P = lluvioso

Q = cubierto (*cloudy*)
S = tormentas
T = templado (*mild*)
V = vientos fuertes (*strong*)

1. ...   2. ...   3. ...   4. ...   5. ...

Vocabulario: Expressing Actions—*hacer*, *poner*, and *salir*

¿Qué hacemos por la noche? Practice telling what you and your acquaintances do in the evening. Use the oral and written cues.

1. Marisol
2. tú
3. los señores Carrasco

4. Vicente y yo
5. yo
6. el profesor de español

Pronunciación y ortografía: *p, t*

A. Like the [k] sound, Spanish [p] and [t] are not aspirated as they are in English. Compare the following pairs of aspirated and nonaspirated English sounds.

pin / spin   pan / span   tan / Stan   top / stop

Repeat the following words, phrases, and sentences, imitating the speaker.

1. pasar   padre   programa   puerta   esperar
2. tienda   todos   traje   estar   usted
3. una tía trabajadora   tres tristes tigres
   un tío tonto   pasar por la puerta
   unos pantalones pardos   un perro perezoso
4. Tomás toma tu té.   Papá paga el papel.
   También toma tu café.   Pero Pablo paga el periódico.

B. *Repaso: [p], [t], [k].* You will hear a series of words. Each will be said twice. Circle the letter of the word you hear.

1. a) pata   b) bata   4. a) dos   b) tos
2. a) van   b) pan   5. a) de   b) té
3. a) coma   b) goma   6. a) callo   b) gallo

Estructuras

14. Expressing Actions: Present Tense of Stem-Changing Verbs

A. *Minidiálogo: Haciendo (making) planes.* You will hear a dialogue followed by a series of statements. Circle the letter of the person who might have made each statement.

1. a) los padres   b) Esteban
2. a) los padres   b) Esteban
3. a) los padres   b) Esteban
4. a) los padres   b) Esteban

B. *Es verano (summer) y hace buen tiempo.* ¿Cuáles son las actividades de todos? Form new sentences, using the oral cues.

1. mi madre   4. yo
2. mi amiga y yo   5. el equipo (*team*)
3. los niños   6. tú

C. *¿Qué haces?* You will hear a series of situations. Each will be said twice. Tell what you might do in each situation, using the present tense of one of these verbs and adding details, if you like. Follow the model. First, listen to the list of verb phrases.

jugar al tenis afuera   servir el café
dormir   cerrar mi libro
pensar en el examen   volver a casa

MODELO: (Mañana hay un examen en la clase de química.) →
Pienso en el examen... ¡y tengo miedo!

1. ...   2. ...   3. ...   4. ...

D. *Entrevista.* You will hear a series of questions about the preferences and opinions of your group of friends. Each will be said twice. Answer using the **nosotros** form of the verb. No answer will be given on the tape. (If you prefer, stop the tape and write the answer.)

1. _____

2. _____

3. _____

4. _____

Vocabulario: Los meses y las estaciones del año

A. *¿Cuándo es... ?* Your Peruvian friend Evangelina wants to know when certain events take place, including a birth date, **una fecha de nacimiento.** Answer, using the written cues.

MODELO: (¿Cuándo es el cumpleaños de Nicolás?) Sunday, May 4 →
Es el domingo, cuatro de mayo.

1. Friday, August 10
2. Saturday, November 22
3. Wednesday, April 14

4. February 11, 1899
5. July 4, 1776

B. *La ropa y el clima.* You will hear a series of descriptions of what people are wearing at a particular time of year in the U.S. Tell what the weather might be and how each person might be feeling, based on the description. You will hear a possible answer on the tape.

MODELO: (Jorge lleva traje de baño y está en la playa. Es el quince de julio.) →
Hace sol y Jorge tiene calor.

1. ...   2. ...   3. ...   4. ...

C. *Conversación: Gustos y preferencias.* You will hear a conversation, partially printed in your manual, about someone's favorite season. Then you will participate in a similar conversation. Complete it based on your own experience. No answers will be given on the tape.

—De todas las estaciones, ¿cuál es tu favorita?

—_____

—_____ ¿Por qué?

—_____

Estructuras

15. Describing: Irregular Comparative Adjectives

A. *Más descripciones.* You will hear the following sentences, followed by questions. Answer using a comparison of inequality and the oral cues.

MODELO: Teresa tiene veinte años. (¿Y una persona que tiene cuarenta años?) →
Es mayor.

1. Las películas italianas son buenas.
2. Pablo es joven.
3. Comer demasiado (*too much*) es malo.
4. Unas tiendas son grandes.

B. *Dictado.* You will hear a series of statements. Each will be said twice. Write the missing words.

1. Esta película es _____ que aquélla, (*that one*). Por eso hay _____ _____ cien personas en este cine.

2. Nati tiene _____ hermanos como hermanas. Su hermanito Ángel tiene _____

_____ diez años. Es el _____.

3. En el desierto hace _____ calor durante el día que durante la noche. Durante el día, la

temperatura llega a _____ _____ treinta grados centígrados.

Un poco de todo

A. *Descripción.* You will hear a series of statements. Each will be said twice. Circle *C* if the statement is true according to the drawing or *F* if it is false.

1.

2.

3.

4.

noviembre

marzo

1. C   F
2. C   F
3. C   F

4. C   F
5. C   F

B. *Estrategias: Getting a General Idea About Content.* Many exercises and activities in this manual and in your textbook have asked you to get the main idea or gist of a dialogue or passage. This section will help you practice a strategy for doing that.

In most cases you can predict the information you are most likely to find in a given passage based on its title alone. This is more difficult to do in listening than in reading because in everyday situations you don't have time to "prepare" for a conversation. In a controlled listening situation like this one, it can help to look at an accompanying visual or to read or listen to the questions about the passage *before* you listen to the passage itself.

The title of the passage you are about to hear is as follows:

Éste es el Año del Caballo (*Horse*) en el Calendario Lunar Chino

Jot down two things that you might expect to hear about in the passage. Just writing a key word or concept is enough, and you may write in English.

_____   _____

Now read the true/false items that you will do after listening to the passage. Do not try to answer them now. Just try to get an idea of what the passage will be about.

1. C F   The passage talks about the origins of the Chinese calendar.
2. C F   The passage provides information about the Chinese New Year.
3. C F   The passage lists the names of the animals for which the Chinese years are named.

Here are some words and phrases that will aid your comprehension of the passage.

antes de Cristo   (*before Christ, B.C.*)
acudieron   (*they came, arrived*)

Now listen to the passage. You can do the comprehension items as you listen or at the end. Rewind the tape and listen again if you need to.

C. *Y para terminar... Entrevista.* You will hear a series of questions. Each will be said twice. Answer based on your own experience. No answers will be given on the tape. (If you prefer, stop the tape and write the answers.)

1. _____
2. _____
3. _____
4. _____
5. _____
6. _____
7. _____

CAPÍTULO
8

Vocabulario: ¡Que aprovechen!

A. *Definiciones.* You will hear a series of definitions. Each will be said twice. Circle the letter of the word that is best defined by each. ¡OJO! There may be more than one answer for some definitions.

1. a) el camarero   b) el cocinero   c) el tenedor
2. a) el menú   b) el mantel   c) la bandeja
3. a) el jarro   b) la botella   c) la copa
4. a) el desayuno   b) la cena   c) la servilleta
5. a) el dinero en efectivo   b) la tarjeta de crédito   c) la cuenta
6. a) la cucharita   b) el cuchillo   c) la cuchara

B. *Identificaciones.* Identify the items in the drawing when you hear the corresponding number.

Vocabulario: Expressing Actions— **oír, traer,** and **ver**

A. *¡No vamos a volver a ese restaurante!* You and some friends are at a restaurant, and everything is going wrong. Describe what is happening, using the oral and written cues.

1. nosotros   3. Eva y Ricardo   5. el camarero
2. el camarero   4. yo   6. tú

B. *Entrevista.* You will hear a series of questions about your eating habits and preferences. Each will be said twice. Answer based on your own experience. No answers will be given on the tape. (If you prefer, stop the tape and write the answer.)

1. _____

2. _____

3. _____

4. _____

5. _____

6. _____

Pronunciación y ortografía: *s, z, ce, ci*

A. The [s] sound in Spanish can be spelled several different ways and has several variants, depending on the country or region of origin of the speaker. Listen to the difference between these pronunciations of the [s] sound in two distinct Spanish-speaking areas of the world.*

SPAIN:	Vamos a llamar a Susana este lunes.
LATIN AMERICA:	Vamos a llamar a Susana este lunes.
SPAIN:	Cecilia siempre cena con Alicia.
LATIN AMERICA:	Cecilia siempre cena con Alicia.
SPAIN:	Zaragoza Zurbarán zapatería
LATIN AMERICA:	Zaragoza Zurbarán zapatería

Notice also that in some parts of the Hispanic world, in rapid speech, the [s] sound becomes aspirated at the end of a syllable or word. Listen as the speaker pronounces these sentences.

¿Hasta cuándo vas a estar allí?
Allí están las mujeres.
Los compramos en Las Cruces.
Estos niños están sucios.

B. Repeat the following words and sentences, imitating the speaker.

1. mes   sol   vaso   sopa   sobrinos   servilletas
2. cocina   piscina   ciudad   sucio   cena   cierto
3. azúcar   actriz   azul   razón   perezoso   noviazgo
4. estación   solución   situación   calefacción   contaminación
5. Siempre salgo a cenar con Zoila.
   Ese sitio muy sucio está en esta ciudad.
   No conozco a Luz Mendoza de Pérez.
   Los zapatos de Celia son azules.

Estructuras

16. Expressing Negation: Indefinite and Negative Words

A. *Descripción.* You will hear a series of questions. Answer according to the drawings.

MODELO: (¿Hay algo en la pizarra?) → <u>Sí, hay algo en la pizarra. Hay unas palabras.</u>

---

*The Latin American variant of the [s] sound is used by most speakers in this tape program.

1.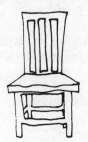

2.

3.

4.

5.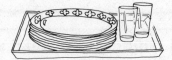

B. *¡Por eso no come nadie allí!* You will hear a series of questions about a very unpopular restaurant. Each will be said twice. Answer using the double negative.

    MODELO: (¿Sirven algunos platos especiales?) → <u>No, no sirven ningún plato especial</u>.

1. ...   2. ...   3. ...   4. ...

C. *Ningún cumpleaños es perfecto.* Using some of the negative words you have learned and the oral cues, tell someone about your worst birthday.

    MODELOS: (cartas) → <u>No hay ninguna carta para mí</u>.
                  (bailar) → <u>Nadie quiere bailar conmigo</u> (*with me*).

1. ...   2. ...   3. ...   4. ...   5. ...

Vocabulario: El inifinitivo—*Preposition + Infinitive*

A. *¿Qué acabas de hacer?* Practice telling what you have just done in the locations you hear on the tape. Choose actions from the following list. First, listen to the list. You will hear a possible answer on the tape.

pedir la cuenta   bailar
comprar un abrigo   regatear con un vendedor (*seller*)
abrir una botella de vino   almorzar con mis amigos

    MODELO: (Estás en la cafetería.) → <u>Acabo de almorzar con mis amigos</u>.

1. ...   2. ...   3. ...   4. ...   5. ...

B. *Situaciones.* You will hear a series of situations. Use **volver a** or **no volver a** to tell what you will say or do in each case. You will hear a possible answer on the tape. Note the meaning of **¿Qué dices?** (*What will you say?*).

> MODELO: Te gusta mucho bailar y estás en una fiesta. Acabas de bailar media hora y estás cansada pero... ¡la música que tocan es muy buena! ¿Qué haces? → ¡Vuelvo a bailar!

1. ...   2. ...   3. ...   4. ...

Estructuras

17. ¿Qué sabes y a quién conoces?: Saber and conocer: Personal a

A. *Minidiálogo: Delante de un restaurante.* You will hear a dialogue followed by a series of statements. Circle the number of the statement that best summarizes the main idea of the dialogue. In this exercise, you will practice listening for the main idea.

1   2   3

B. *¿De veras?* (Really?) You have just made some statements to which your friend Armando reacts with surprise. Respond to his reaction, using **saber** or **conocer**, as appropriate.

> MODELO: (¿Tú? ¿jugar al básquetbol?) → Sí, sé jugar muy bien al básquetbol.

1. ...   2. ...   3. ...   4. ...

C. *En un restaurante ruidoso* (noisy). Your friend Margarita has made a series of statements and you haven't quite understood everything she said. Ask her questions based on each statement, using **¿qué?, ¿a quién?,** or **¿a quiénes?,** as appropriate.

> MODELO: (Veo a los señores Garza.) → ¿A quiénes ves?

1. ...   2. ...   3. ...   4. ...   5. ...

D. *Entrevista.* You will hear a series of questions about yourself. Each will be said twice. Answer based on your own experience. No answers will be given on the tape. (If you prefer, stop the tape and write the answer.)

1. _____

2. _____

3. _____

4. _____

5. _____

6. _____

Un poco de todo

A. *Listening Passage.* You will hear a brief passage about the typical bars found in Madrid where **entremeses**, light snacks or hors d'oeuvres, are served. Then you will hear a series of incomplete statements about the passage. Complete each statement based on the listening passage.

1. a) tapas
2. a) después de (*after*) almorzar
3. a) bistec con patatas
4. a) regatear

b) tascas
b) después de salir del teatro
b) entremeses o tapas
b) escuchar música

B. *Y para terminar... Descripción.* Which drawing is best defined by the statements you hear? Each will be said twice.

1. a)  b)

2. a)  b)

3. a)  b)

4. a)  b)

Un paso más: Situaciones

A. *En un restaurante español.* In the following conversation, you will hear how to order from a menu. Read the dialogue silently, along with the speakers.

MANUEL:	¿Nos sentamos? Creo que aquí se está bien.
ANA MARÍA:	Perfecto. Aquí viene el camarero. ¿Por qué no pides tú la cena ya que conoces este restaurante?
CAMARERO:	Buenas noches, señores. ¿Desean algo de aperitivo?
MANUEL:	Para la señorita, un vermut; para mí, un vino. Los trae con jamón, queso y anchoas°, por favor. ¿Y qué recomienda Ud. de comida?
CAMARERO:	El solomillo a la parrilla° es la especialidad de la casa. Como plato del día hay paella...
MANUEL:	Bueno. De entrada, el gazpacho°. De plato fuerte, el solomillo con patatas y guisantes. Ensalada de lechuga y tomate. Y de postre, flan°. Vino tinto y, al final, dos cafés.
ANA MARÍA:	Manolo, basta ya. ¡Estoy a dieta y he merendado más de la cuenta°!
MANUEL:	Chica, ¿qué importa? Luego vamos a bailar.

jamón...ham, cheese, and anchovies

solomillo...grilled filet mignon

chilled tomato soup

de... for dessert, custard

he...I have snacked more than I should have

Now it's your turn to order. The same waiter will ask you questions about each part of the meal. Answer based on the dialogue or based on your own preferences. You will hear a possible answer on the tape. The waiter will continue after you repeat the answer.

1. ...   2. ...   3. ...   4. ...

B. *En un restaurante.* Using the following expressions, tell the same waiter you have been talking to what you need or need to know. You will hear a possible answer on the tape. The waiter will respond after you repeat the answer. First, listen to the list of expressions.

¿Qué recomienda Ud.?   Favor de traerme (una servilleta).
Me trae (un vaso), por favor.

1. ...   2. ...   3. ...   4. ...

REPASO

2

A. *En el periódico: Espectáculos.* You will hear a brief article that appeared in a Spanish newspaper. Then you will hear two statements. Circle the number of the statement that best summarizes the article. In this exercise, you will practice gisting (listening for the main idea).

1   2

B. *En el periódico.* You will hear a brief article about a prize won by a group of people in Spain. It will be read twice. Listen carefully and circle the numbers you hear. In this exercise, you will practice listening for specific information.

1   2   5   6   8   12   100   10.000   34.000   134.000.000

Now listen to the article again. Circle the number of the word or words with which you associate the article. Try not to be distracted by unfamiliar vocabulary, and see if you can get the gist of the article.

1. los libros	3. el dinero
2. la lotería	4. la policía

C. *De compras con Sergio.* You will hear a paragraph that describes a sequence of events. Listen carefully and number the drawings in the following series from 1 to 5, according to the sequence of events described in the paragraph. One of the drawings does not belong at all. Cross it out. First, look at the drawings. In this exercise, you will practice listening for specific information, as well as putting events into the correct sequence. Note the meaning of these words.

antes de (*before*)
después de (*after*)

a. ___   b. ___   c. ___

d. ___   e. ___   f. ___

D. *Situaciones: ¡Buen viaje!* Imagine that you will travel to a variety of places this year. Answer the questions you hear about each of your trips, using the written cues. ¡OJO! The questions may vary slightly from those seen in the model. Change your answers accordingly. You will hear a possible answer on the tape.

> MODELO: March 30 / 2 / impermeable
> (¿Cuándo sales para Seattle?) → <u>Salgo el treinta de marzo</u>.
> (¿Cuántas semanas vas a estar allí?) → <u>Creo que dos</u>.
> (¿No llueve mucho en Seattle?) → <u>Sí. Por eso voy a llevar mi impermeable</u>.

1. December 15 / 3 / traje de baño
2. February 29 / 1 / camisetas
3. September 1 / 2 / suéteres

E. *Descripción: La boda de Marisol y Gregorio.* Using the written cues, describe what you see in this drawing after you hear the name of each person or item. When more than one choice is given, choose the word that best describes the situation. You will hear a possible answer on the tape.

1. ser / estar contento / triste
2. llevar guapo / feo / bonito
3. ser / estar mesa
4. pedir / traer el champán
5. ser / estar tan / más / menos alto Gregorio
6. ser / estar hermano menor / mayor Marisol

F. *Descripción.* You will hear a series of questions. Each will be said twice. Base your answers on the following cartoon. You will hear a possible answer on the tape.

The following words appear in the questions or are useful for answering them. Listen to them before the questions are read.

una taza (*cup*)
veces (*times, occasions*)
al final (*in the end*)
por fin (*finally*)

Now look briefly at the cartoon.

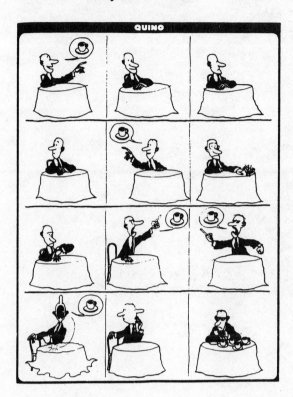

1. ...   2. ...   3. ...   4. ...   5. ...   6. ...

G. *Entrevista.* You will hear a series of questions about yourself, the weather, and where you live. Each will be said twice. Answer based on your own experience. No answers will be given on the tape. (If you prefer, stop the tape and write the answer.)

1. _____

2. _____

3. _____

4. _____

5. _____

6. _____

7. _____

8. _____

9. _____

CAPÍTULO

9

Vocabulario: La comida y las bebidas

A. *¿Qué va a pedir Juan?* Juan and his friend Marta are in a restaurant. Listen to their conversation and circle the items that Juan is going to order. In this exercise, you will practice listening for specific information.

B. *Identificaciones*. Identify the following foods when you hear the corresponding number. Use the definite article in your answer.

C. *¿Cuándo comes? ¿Qué comiste ayer?* You will be asked at what time you generally eat your meals and what you ate yesterday at each meal. Each will be said twice. Answer based on your own experience. You will hear a possible answer on the tape.

1. ...
2. Comí...

3. ...
4. Comí...

5. ...
6. Comí...

Pronunciación y ortografía: *j, g, gu*

A. The [x] sound can be written as *j* (before all vowels) or as *g* (before *e* and *i*). Its pronunciation varies, depending on the region or country of origin of the speaker. Note the difference in the pronunciation of these words.

| España: | Jorge | jueves | gente | álgebra |
| el Caribe: | Jorge | jueves | gente | álgebra |

B. Repeat the following words and phrases, imitating the speaker.

1. Jalisco jirafa fijo extranjero mujer joven viejo consejera
2. general generoso inteligente geografía región religión sicología
3. una región geográfica
   una mujer generosa
   un consejero joven

C. The [g] sound is written as *g* before the vowels *a, o,* and *u* and as *gu* before *e* and *i*. In addition, it has two variants. At the beginning of a word, after a pause, or after n, it is pronounced like the *g* in *get*. In all other positions, it has a softer sound produced by allowing some air to escape when it is pronounced. There is no exact equivalent for this second variant in English.

Repeat the following words and sentences, imitating the speaker.

1. [g] grande tengo gusto gracias guapo ganga
2. [g̵] amiga diálogo pagar regatear delgado el gorila
3. ¿Cuánto pagaste?
   ¡Qué ganga!   Domingo es guapo y delgado.   Tengo algunas amigas guatemaltecas.

D. *Dictado*. You will hear four sentences. Each will be said twice. Listen carefully and write what you hear.

1. _____

2. _____

3. _____

4. _____

Estructuras

18. Expressing *What* or *Whom*: Direct Object Pronouns

A. *Minidiálogo: ¿Dónde vamos a comer?* You will hear a dialogue followed by two statements about the dialogue. Circle the number of the statement that best summarizes what happens in the dialogue. In this dialogue, you will practice listening for the main idea.

1   2

B. *En la cocina* (kitchen). You are preparing a meal, and your friend Pablo is in the kitchen helping you. Answer his questions, using object pronouns and the written cues. You will hear each question twice.

MODELO: (¿Necesitas la olla [*pan*] ahora?)
          sí → <u>¿La olla? Sí, la necesito</u>.
          no → <u>¿La olla? No, no la necesito todavía</u>.

1. no		4. no	
2. sí		5. sí	
3. sí			

C. *Descripción: ¿Qué hacen estas personas?* You will hear a series of questions. Answer based on the drawings. Follow the model.

MODELO: ¿Toma el pedido [*the order*] un camarero? → <u>Sí, lo toma</u>.

1. ...   2. ...   3. ...   4. ...   5. ...

D. *Entre amigos...* Your friend Manuel, who hasn't seen you for a while (**hace tiempo...**), wants to know when the two of you can get together again. Answer his questions using the written cues. You will hear each question twice.

1. lunes		3. 4:00
2. para esta tarde		4. Café Gijón

Vocabulario: ¿Dónde está?—Las preposiciones

Descripción: En un cóctel. Describe a cocktail party at which you are a guest by answering the questions you hear based on the drawing. Each will be said twice. You will hear a possible answer on the tape.

1. ...   2. ...   3. ...   4. ...   5. ...   6. ...

Estructuras

19. Getting Information: Summary of Interrogative Words

A. *¿Qué dijiste?* (What did you say?) You and your friend Eva are at a noisy party. She has just made several statements, but you haven't understood everything she said. You will hear each statement only once. Choose an appropriate interrogative word and form a question to elicit the information you need. Eva will answer your questions.

MODELO: (Llegan mañana.)   a) ¿dónde?   b) ¿cuándo? → b → ¿Cuándo llegan? (Mañana.)

1. a) ¿de quién?   b) ¿quién?
2. a) ¿quién?   b) ¿quiénes?
3. a) ¿de dónde?   b) ¿adónde?
4. a) ¿cuál?   b) ¿qué?
5. a) ¿cuántos?   b) ¿cuánto?
6. a) ¿cuál?   b) ¿qué?

B. *Entrevista con la señorita Moreno.* Interview Ms. Moreno, an exchange student, for your school newspaper, using the written cues. Add any necessary words. You will hear the correct question, as well as her answer.

MODELO: ¿dónde? / ser → Srta. Moreno, ¿de dónde es Ud.? (Soy de Chile.)

1. ¿dónde? / vivir   4. ¿qué? / instrumento musical
2. ¿dónde? / trabajar   5. ¿cuánto? / hermanos
3. ¿qué? / idiomas

Un poco de todo

A. *En el restaurante El Charro.* You are in a Mexican restaurant and the waiter is asking you what you would like to eat. Use the following menu and the written cues to make your choices. You will hear a possible answer on the tape. First, look at the menu.

Menú - El Charro

Antojitos ~
Cóctel de camarones
Nachos
Guacamole

Sopas ~
Sopa de tortillas
Sopa de pescado

Platos principales ~
Mole poblano de guajolote
Tacos "El Charro"
Bistec con papas fritas

Postres ~
Helado de chocolate ☆
Flan ☆ Fruta ☆

Bebidas ~ Vino (tinto, blanco o rosado) ☆ Cerveza ☆
Agua mineral ☆ Café ☆ Té ☆

---

1. Favor de traerme...
2. Sí. Me trae... , por favor
3. ¿Todavía hay... ?

4. Entonces, me trae... , por favor
5. Quiero... , por favor
6. Favor de traerme...

B. *Estrategias: Words with Multiple Meanings.* In listening, as well as in reading, your ability to understand can be affected by words with multiple meanings. For example, the word **esperar** can mean *to hope for*, *to wait for*, or *to expect*. The context will determine the correct meaning.

Here is a list of some other Spanish words with multiple meanings.

como	=	I eat; like; as; since; the way that
que	=	that, who, whom
clase	=	class meeting; course; type
paso	=	step; dance step; I pass; I stop by
peso	=	I weigh; weight; monetary unit

You will hear a series of brief conversations. Each one contains a Spanish word that has multiple meanings. Listen carefully and circle the meaning that is appropriate according to context. ¡OJO! Nouns may not always be in the singular form.

1. a) I weigh
2. a) I weigh
3. a) I will stop by
4. a) I will stop by
5. a) I eat

b) monetary unit
b) monetary unit
b) step
b) step
b) since

c) weight
c) weight
c) dance step
c) dance step
c) like

C. *Y para terminar... En el periódico: Guía* (Guide) *de restaurantes.* The following ads for restaurants appeared in a Spanish newspaper. Use them to answer the questions you will hear. First look at the ads.

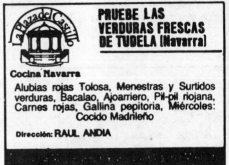

PRUEBE LAS VERDURAS FRESCAS DE TUDELA (Navarra)

Cocina Navarra

Alubias rojas Tolosa, Menestras y Surtidos verduras, Bacalao, Ajoarriero, Pil-pil riojana, Carnes rojas, Gallina pepitoria, Miércoles: Cocido Madrileño

Dirección: RAUL ANDIA

NUEVO RESTAURANTE JUAN AGUSTIN
COCINA de TEMPORADA
Ameniza al Piano
el Maestro POSADAS
Jefe de Cocina **JUAN AGUSTIN**
San Leonardo, 12–(Pza. España)
Tels. 241 55 88–248 49 49
(Cerrado domingos)

BAR-RESTAURANTE

PRIMERA CASA EN MARISCOS

ESPECIALIDADES:
PESCADOS, AHUMADOS, JAMON DE JABUGO

NARVAEZ, 68   273 10 67
MADRID   273 82 98

1. ...   2. ...   3. ...   4. ...   5. ...

CAPÍTULO

10

Vocabulario: En el aeropuerto

A. *Situaciones: De viaje.* You will hear a series of situations. Each will be said twice. Circle the letter of the best solution or response for each.

1. a) Salgo en dos semanas.
   b) Compro un boleto de ida y vuelta.
   c) Compro un boleto de ida.
2. a) ¡Estoy aburrido!
   b) ¡Estoy atrasado!
   c) ¡Estoy cansado!
3. a) Pido un pasaje de primera clase.
   b) Bajo del avión.
   c) Viajo en clase turística.
4. a) Pedimos asientos en la clase turística.
   b) Pedimos asientos en la sección de fumar.
   c) Pedimos asientos en la sección de no fumar.
5. a) Hago cola.
   b) Despego a tiempo.
   c) Lo facturo.

B. *Identificaciones.* Identify the items after you hear the corresponding number. Begin each sentence with **Es...** or **Son...** and the appropriate indefinite article.

1. ...   2. ...   3. ...   4. ...   5. ...   6. ...   7. ...   8. ...

C. *Hablando de viajes...* Using the oral and written cues, tell your friend Benito, who has never traveled by plane, the steps he should follow to make an airplane trip.

MODELO: Primero... (llamar a la agencia de viajes) → <u>Primero llamas a la agencia de viajes</u>.

1. pedir
2. El día del viaje,...
3. facturar

4. Después...
5. Cuando anuncian la salida del vuelo,...
6. Por fin (*finally*)...

Pronunciación y ortografía: *ñ, ch*

A. The pronunciation of the *ñ* is similar to the sound [ny] in the English words *canyon* and *union*. However, in Spanish it is pronounced as one single sound.

Repeat the following words and sentences, imitating the speaker.

1. cana / caña   sonar / soñar   mono / moño   tino / tiño   cena / seña
2. año   señora   cañón   español   pequeña   compañero
3. El señor Muñoz es de España.
   Los niños pequeños no enseñan español.
   La señorita Ordóñez tiene veinte años.

B. You will hear a series of words. Circle the letter of the word you hear.

1. a) pena   b) peña
2. a) una   b) uña
3. a) lena   b) leña

4. a) suena   b) sueña
5. a) mono   b) moño

C. In Spanish, the letter *ch* is pronounced like its English equivalent in *church*. Read the following words when you hear the corresponding number; then repeat the correct pronunciation.

1. mucho
2. muchacho
3. Concha

4. Chile
5. mochila
6. hache

D. *Dictado.* You will hear four sentences. Each will be said twice. Write what you hear.

1. _____

2. _____

3. _____

4. _____

Estructuras

20. Expressing *to whom* or *for whom*: Indirect Object Pronouns: **dar** and **decir**

A. *Minidiálogo: En la sala de espera del aeropuerto.* You will hear a dialogue followed by a series of statements. Circle *C* if the statement is true or *F* if it is false. In this exercise, you will practice listening for specific information.

1. C F   2. C F   3. C F   4. C F

B. *En casa durante la cena.* Practice telling for whom the following things are being done, according to the model.

MODELO: Mi padre sirve el guacamole. (a nosotros) → <u>Mi padre nos sirve el guacamole.</u>

1. Mi madre sirve la sopa.
2. Ahora ella prepara la ensalada.
3. Mi hermano trae el café.
4. Rosalinda da postre.

C. *Descripción.* When you hear the corresponding number, tell what the people indicated are doing. Use the written cues with indirect object pronouns.

En la fiesta de aniversario de los Sres. Moreno

1. Susana: regalar   2. Miguel: mandar   3. Tito: regalar

En casa, durante el desayuno

4. Pedro: dar   5. Marta: dar   6. Luis: servir

D. *Preguntas.* Practice telling about things we do for others and things others do for us. Each will be said twice. Answer, using the written cues.

1. hermano menor
2. compañera de cuarto
3. mejores amigos

4. mi novia
5. mejor amigo
6. amigos

Estructuras

21. Expressing Likes and Dislikes: **Gustar**

A. *Descripción: Parece que a Ud. no le gusta el humo* (smoke). You will hear a series of questions. Answer based on the drawing and your own experience. You will hear a possible answer on the tape.

1. ...   2. ...   3. ...   4. ...

B. *¿Qué le gusta? ¿Qué odia?* Using the written cues, practice telling what you like, dislike, or hate about the following situations or locations. You will hear a possible answer on the tape.

MODELOS: En la universidad: fiestas / exámenes →
           Me gustan las fiestas, pero odio los exámenes.
           En una discoteca: la música / las bebidas →
           Me gustan la música y las bebidas.

1. En la playa: sol / agua
2. En un restaurante: comida / música
3. En un parque: insectos / flores
4. En una pastelería (*pastry shop*): chocolates / caramelos
5. En el aeropuerto: volar en avión / demoras

C. *Dictado: Una celebración.* You will hear the following paragraphs. Listen carefully and write the missing words. Rewind the tape and listen again if you need to.

Anita y Julio _____ [1] ir a _____ [2] fuera esta noche porque _____ [3] el

cumpleaños de _____. [4] Anita hace reservaciones en el restaurante _____ [5] que está

cerca de su apartamento _____ [6] es el restaurante favorito de su _____. [7] A

_____ [8] le _____ [9] mucho la comida mexicana.

Cuando Anita y Julio _____ [10] al restaurante, el camarero _____ [11] enseña la

_____ [12] reservada, pero no _____ [13] gusta porque está _____ [14] cerca de la

_____. [15] Por fin encuentran una que _____ [16] _____ [17] situada y

_____ [18] piden el menú _____ [19] camarero. Después de _____, [20] Anita y

Julio _____ [21] indican al camarero lo que _____ [22] comer. Él _____ [23] trae la

comida y les dice «¡Buen provecho!» (*"Enjoy your meal!"*)

_____ [24] de cenar, Anita _____ [25] pide dos cafés y _____ [26] de chocolate

_____ [27] camarero. Él _____ [28] trae con la _____. [29]

Después de _____, [30] Anita le pregunta a Julio si le _____ [31] ir a bailar. Para Julio,

fue un _____ [32] muy feliz!

Now you will hear a series of statements based on the preceding paragraph. Each will be said twice. Circle *C* if the statement is true or *F* if it is false.

1. C F   2. C F   3. C F   4. C F   5. C F

D. *Entrevista: Gustos y preferencias.* You will hear a series of questions. Each will be said twice. Answer based on your own experience. No answers will be given on the tape. (If you prefer, stop the tape and write the answer.)

1. _____

2. _____

3. _____

4. _____

5. _____

6. _____

Un poco de todo

A. *En el periódico: Anuncios.* You will hear an ad for a Mexican airline company. Then you will hear a series of statements. Circle *C* if the statement is true or *F* if it is false based on the information contained in the ad and the following chart of departures.

MIAMI 10 vuelos semanales

SALIDAS	LUNES	MARTES	MIERCOLES	JUEVES	VIERNES	SABADO	DOMINGO
	11:50 Y 15:05	16:10	11:50 Y 16:10	15:15	11:50 Y 11:05	15:15	15:05

1. C F   2. C F   3. C F   4. C F

B. *Listening Passage: Anuncio turístico.* You will hear a brief travel ad. Then you will hear a series of statements about the ad. Circle **C** if the statement is true or **F** if it is false.

1. C F   2. C F   3. C F   4. C F

C. *Y para terminar. Descripción: En el avión.* You will hear a series of questions. Each will be said twice. Answer, based on the drawing. You will hear a possible answer on the tape. First, look at the drawing.

1. ...   2. ...   3. ...   4. ...   5. ...   6. ...

Un paso más: Situaciones

A. *Se busca transporte.* The following conversation shows how to arrange for transportation when traveling by plane. Read it silently, along with the speakers.

En el aeropuerto

—Buenas tardes, señor.
—Muy buenas. Aquí están mi boleto y mi pasaporte.
—Perfecto. ¿Éste es todo el equipaje que va a facturar?
—Sí, sólo esas dos maletas.
—Y ¿dónde quiere sentarse?
—Me gustaría estar en la sección de los no fumadores. Quiero la ventanilla y lo más adelante posible, por favor.
—Muy bien. Tiene el asiento 23A. Ya puede seguir a la puerta de embarque número 7. El vuelo está atrasado veinticinco minutos solamente.

B. Now you will hear another conversation, partially printed in your manual, about arranging for train transportation. Then you will participate in a similar conversation. Complete it with the cues suggested. You will hear a possible answer on the tape.

—_____. Me da _____ .

—¿Para qué tren? Hay un tren a _____, uno a _____ y otro a _____.

—Déme uno para el tren de _____.

—Lo siento, pero ya no hay boletos para _____.

—Entonces, _____ .

CAPÍTULO

11

Vocabulario: ¡Vamos de vacaciones!

A. *Definiciones*. You will hear a series of definitions. Each will be said twice. Circle the letter of the word that is best defined by each. ¡OJO! There may be more than one answer in some cases.

1. a) el avión   b) la playa   c) el océano
2. a) la casa   b) el desierto   c) el océano
3. a) el terminal   b) la estación de trenes   c) el aeropuerto
4. a) el hotel   b) el restaurante   c) el crucero
5. a) volar   b) navegar   c) nadar

B. *¿Qué les gusataría hacer para sus vacaciones?* You will hear descriptions of what four different people like. Write the number of the description next to the type of activity you think each person would prefer to do on his or her vacation. ¡OJO! There are two extra activities. First, listen to the list of activities.

___ montar a caballo

___ jugar al golf

___ estar en casa

___ navegar en barco

___ nadar

___ ir a las montañas

C. *Entrevista.* You will hear a series of questions about what you and others in general do on vacation. Each will be said twice. Answer based on your own experience. You will hear a possible answer on the tape. (If you prefer, stop the tape and write the answer.)

1. _____
2. _____
3. _____
4. _____
5. _____
6. _____

Pronunciación y ortografía: *y* and *ll*

A. At the beginning of a word of syllable, the Spanish sound *y* is pronounced somewhat like the letter *y* in English *yo-yo* or *papaya*. However, there is no exact English equivalent for this sound. In addition, there are variants of the sound, depending on the country of origin of the speaker.

Listen to these differences:

    el Caribe: Yolanda lleva una blusa amarilla. Yo no.
      España: Yolanda lleva una blusa amarilla. Yo no.
  la Argentina: Yolanda lleva una blusa amarilla. Yo no.

B. Although *y* and *ll* are pronounced exactly the same by most Spanish speakers, in some regions of Spain *ll* is pronounced like the [y] sound in *million*, except that it is one single sound.

Listen to these differences:

      España: Guillermo es de Castilla.
  Sudamérica: Guillermo es de Castilla.

C. Repeat the following words, imitating the speaker.

1. llamo   llueve   yogurt   yate   yanqui   yoga
2. ellas   tortilla   millón   mayo   destruyo   oye

D. *¿Ll o l?* You will hear a series of words. Each will be said twice. Circle the letter used to spell each.

1. ll l   3. ll l   5. ll l
2. ll l   4. ll l   6. ll l

E. *Repaso: ñ, ll, y.* When you hear the corresponding number, read the following sentences. Then listen to the correct pronunciation and say the sentence again.

1. El señor Muñoz es de España y habla español.
2. Yolanda Carrillo es de Castilla.
3. ¿Llueve o no llueve allá en Yucatán?

Estructuras

22. Influencing Others: Present Subjunctive: An Introduction

A. *Minidiálogo: Un pasajero distraído.* You will hear a dialogue followed by a series of statements about the dialogue. Circle *C* if the statement is true or *F* if it is false. In this exercise, you will practice listening for specific information.

1. C F   2. C F   3. C F   4. C F

B. Repeat the following verb phrases, imitating the speaker.

1. que cante   que cantes   que cantemos   que canten
2. que diga   que digas   que digamos   que digan
3. que pague   que pagues   que paguemos   que paguen
4. que empiece   que empieces   que empecemos   que empiecen
5. que vaya   que vayas   que vayamos   que vayan
6. que duerma   que duermas   que durmamos   que duerman

C. *Antes del viaje: ¿Qué quiere Ud. que hagan estas personas?* You are traveling with a large group of students. Using the oral and written cues, tell each person what you want him or her to do.

MODELO: Jorge (hacer las maletas) → <u>Quiero que Jorge haga las maletas</u>.

1. Toño   3. Ana y Teresa   5. todos
2. Alberto   4. todos   6. todos

D. *Dictado: De vacaciones.* You will hear a series of sentences. Each will be said twice. Listen carefully and write the missing words.

1. El inspector _____ que los turistas _____ _____ los pasaportes.

2. Paquita y yo _____ que _____ con nosotras.

3. El Sr. Hurtado _____ que su esposa _____ al tenis.

4. Antonio _____ que _____ en un barco.

Vocabulario: Expressing Wishes—¡Ojalá!

Hablemos (*Let's talk*) **de deseos.** Tell what you would like to see happen in the world some day, based on the written cues. Express your wish when you hear the corresponding number, beginning your wishes with **Ojalá que...** . You will hear a possible answer on the tape.

1. no hay guerras (*wars*)
2. todos / tener un hogar (casa)
3. nosotros / poder resolver el problema del hambre
4. hay igualdad (*equality*) para todos

Estructuras

23. Asking Someone to Do Something: Formal Commands

A. *¿Qué acaban de decir?* You will hear a series of commands. Write the number of the command you hear next to the corresponding drawing. You will hear each command twice. ¡OJO! There is an extra drawing.

a) ___

b) ___

c) ___

d) ___

e) ___

B. *Profesora por un día...* You are the Spanish professor for the day. Practice telling your students what they should do, using the oral cues. Use **Uds.** commands.

1. ...   2. ...   3. ...   4. ...   5. ...

C. *Consejos y mandatos.* You will hear a series of situations followed by questions. Each will be said twice. Answer each using an appropriate command based on phrases from the following list. You will hear a possible answer on the tape. First, listen to the list.

(no) dormir más
(no) comer tantos postres
(no) llamarlos por teléfono

(no) fumar aquí
(no) viajar en avión
(no) hablar en español

> MODELO: (La señorita Alonso es profesora de español. ¿Qué les aconseja ella a los estudiantes de su clase?) → <u>Hablen Uds. en español</u>.

1. ...   2. ...   3. ...   4. ...   5. ...

Un poco de todo

A. *Conversación: ¡Por fin estamos de vacaciones!* You will hear a conversation, partially printed in your manual, about vacation plans. Then you will participate in a similar conversation about your own vacation plans. Complete it based on your own experience. No answers will be given on the tape.

—¿Cuántos días te dan de vacaciones?

—Este año,_____

—¿Vas a ir a algún lugar?

—¡Claro! Es posible que _____

B. *Estrategias: More About Getting the General Idea.* You have already practiced predicting the information that might appear in a listening passage or article, on the basis of the title of the materials. You will practice that technique again here, as well as guess the meaning of some words from context.

The title of the ad you are about to hear is **Vacaciones en Margarita.** Without looking at the ad, jot down four things you might expect to find in the ad. Just writing a key word or concept is enough, and you may write in English.

_____   _____

_____   _____

Now scan the list of words you will be asked to find in the ad after listening to the passage. Do not try to give them now.

¿Como se dice en español?

1. towels
2. air conditioning
3. rental
4. occupancy

¿Cierto o falso?

1. C F   2. C F   3. C F   4. C F

C. *Y para terminar... Entrevista: Hablando de vacaciones.* You will hear a series of questions about your vacation plans. Each will be said twice. Answer according to your own experience. No answers will be given on the tape. (If you prefer, stop the tape and write the answer.)

1. _____

2. _____

3. _____

4. _____

_Nombre_____ _Fecha_ _____ _Clase_____

Vocabulario: Tengo... Necesito... Quiero... Los bienes personales

A. *Hablando de lo que necesitamos*. You will hear a brief dialogue between two friends, Lidia and Daniel. Listen carefully and circle the items that are mentioned in their conversation. Don't be distracted by unfamiliar vocabulary. First, take time to look at the drawing.

B. *Definiciones*. You will hear a series of statements. Each will be said twice. Circle the letter of the word that is best defined by each.

1. a) el trofeo
2. a) el grabador de vídeo
3. a) la motocicleta
4. a) la cámara
5. a) el sueldo
6. a) el acuario

    b) los impuestos
    b) el compact disc
    b) la camioneta
    b) la impresora
    b) el jefe
    b) la piscina

C. *Entrevista*. You will hear a series of questions about what you own or what interests you. Each will be said twice. Answer based on your own experience. You will hear a possible answer on the tape. (If you prefer, stop the tape and write the answer.)

1. _____
2. _____
3. _____
4. _____
5. _____

Pronunciación y ortografía: *x, n*

A. The letter *x* is usually pronounced [ks] as in English. Before a consonant, however, it is often pronounced [s]. Repeat the following words, imitating the speaker.

1. [ks] léxico   sexo   axial   existen   examen
2. [s] explican   extraordinario   extremo   sexto   extraterrestre
3. ¿Piensas que existen los extraterrestres?
   ¡Nos explican que es algo extraordinario!
   No me gustan las temperaturas extremas.
   La medicina no es una ciencia exacta.

B. Before *p, b, v,* and *m,* the letter *n* is pronounced [m]. Before the sounds [k], [g], and [x], *n* is pronounced like the [ng] sound in the English word *sing*. In all other positions, *n* is pronounced as it is in English.

Repeat the following words and phrases, imitating the speaker.

1. [m] convence   un beso   un peso   con Manuel   con Pablo   en Perú   en Venezuela   en México   son buenos
2. [ng] en casa   en Castilla   un general   son generosos   son jóvenes   en Quito   en Granada   con Juan

Estructuras

24. Expressing Desires and Requests: The Subjunctive in Noun Clauses: Concepts; Influence

A. *Minidiálogo: El viernes, por la tarde.* You will hear a dialogue followed by three statements. Circle the number of the statement that best summarizes the dialogue. In this exercise, you will practice getting the main idea.

1   2   3

B. *¿Qué recomienda el nuevo jefe?* You have a new boss in your office and he is determined to make some changes. Tell what he recommends, using the written and oral cues.

MODELO: no llegar tarde: yo (recomendar) → <u>El jefe recomienda que no llegue tarde</u>.

1. buscar otro puesto: Ud.
2. trabajar hasta muy tarde: todos
3. dormir en la oficina: Federico
4. ser puntuales: nosotros
5. fumar en la oficina: tú

Now you will hear a series of questions about the boss whose requests you have just described. Each will be said twice. Answer based on your own opinions. No answer will be given on the tape.

1. ...   2. ...   3. ...

C. *Preparativos para un viaje en tren.* Your Spanish friends are going on vacation to Germany. They have never been out of the country before. Answer their questions, using object pronouns when possible, but don't try to use both direct and indirect object pronouns in the same sentence. You will hear each question twice.

   MODELO: (¿Tenemos que hacer reservaciones?) → <u>Sí, es necesario que las hagan</u>.

1. ...   2. ...   3. ...   4. ...

D. *Entrevista: ¿Cómo es el trabajo ideal?* Here is your chance to describe the perfect job. Answer the following questions about the characteristics that job would have. Each question will be asked twice. You will hear a possible answer on the tape. (If you prefer, stop the tape and write the answer.)

1. _____

2. _____

3. _____

4. _____

5. _____

Notas Lingüísticas: More About Describing Things

¿Qué esperan estas personas? You will hear brief descriptions of four individuals. Tell what you think each person might hope to receive as a gift, based on the information in each description. Begin your answers with **Quiere que le den...** and choose items from the following list (or suggest others). You will hear a possible answer on the tape. First, listen to the list. There are two extra items.

un anillo de oro   un grabador de vídeo
un suéter de lana   una camiseta de algodón
un reloj de plata   unos platos de plástico

   MODELO: Quiere que le den...

1. ...   2. ...   3. ...   4. ...

Estructuras

25. Expressing Feelings: The Subjunctive in Noun Clauses: Emotion

A. *Minidiálogo: Un futuro peatón.* You will hear a dialogue followed by two statements. Circle the number of the statement that best summarizes the dialogue. You will practice listening for the main idea.

1   2

B. *Sentimientos.* Practice telling how you feel about the following things, using the oral cues. Add any necessary words.

MODELO: no venir nadie a mi fiesta (tener miedo) →
Tengo miedo de que no venga nadie a mi fiesta.

1. mis padres / estar bien
2. mi auto / no funcionar
3. haber una crisis mundial

4. mis amigos / llamarme con frecuencia
5. tú / no tener trabajo

C. *Comentarios sobre el mundo del trabajo.* Your friend Nuria will make a series of statements, which are printed in your manual. React to her statements using the oral cues.

MODELO: La jefa va a renunciar a (*resign from*) su puesto. (es extraño) →
Es extraño que la jefa renuncie a su puesto.

1. Los empleados reciben un buen sueldo.
2. El jefe piensa despedir a Anita.

3. El director hace un viaje a Europa.
4. La abogada (*lawyer*) habla español.

D. *Descripción: Esperanzas* (hopes) *y temores* (fears). You will hear two questions about each drawing. Answer based on the drawings and the written cues. You will hear a possible answer on the tape.

1. sacar (*to get*) malas notas (*grades*) / sacar una A
2. darle un aumento / despedirla
3. haber regalos para él / no haber nada para él

Un poco de todo

A. *El mundo laboral.* You will hear a dialogue followed by a series of statements. Circle the letter of the person who might have made each statement.

1. a) el jefe   b) Álvaro
2. a) el jefe   b) Álvaro
3. a) el jefe   b) Álvaro
4. a) el jefe   b) Álvaro

B. *Listening Passage.* The following brief interview with a Spanish businesswoman points out some of the differences in business hours between the United States and Spain. Then you will hear a series of statements about the interview. Circle *C* if the statement is true or *F* if it is false.

1. C F   2. C F   3. C F   4. C F

C. *Y para terminar... En el periódico: Clasificados.* The following ads appeared in Hispanic newspapers. Decide which item you would most like to purchase and answer the questions. If the ad for the item you wish to purchase does not have the information asked for in the questions, say **No lo dice.** No answers will be given on the tape. First, look at the ad for the item you want to buy.

1.

2.

PIANOS

Las mas famosas marcas

de todo el el mundo !

Al Interior en 24 hs. Estacionam. Propio

Planes de 3 a 40 MESES !

Incluye en su compra: ALBUM 100 temas, CURSO familiar privado, AURICULARES de luxe y material didáctico !

REPRESENTANTES

ChOPIN

de CARNEVALE Hnos

MEMBRILLAR 68 - Cap.
Alt. Av. Rivadavia al 6800
Lun/Sáb. 9 a 21. Domingos
Abierto de 16 a 20

ORGANOS

LOGAN-CASIO
GEM-TECHNICS

1. ...   2. ...   3. ...   4. ...   5. ...

REPASO

3

A. You will hear five brief conversations or parts of conversations. Write the number of each conversation in the appropriate blank to indicate where it might have taken place. First, listen to the locations.

___ un restaurante   ___ un crucero

___ un avión   ___ una oficina

___ la estación del tren   ___ la sala de espera de un aeropuerto

B. *Estrategias: Repaso:* Words with Multiple Meanings. You will hear a series of sentences. Each will be said twice. For each sentence, circle the letter of the meaning of the indicated word according to the context of the sentence. First, listen to the words.

		a)	b)	c)
1.	como:	I eat	how	like
2.	equipo:	I equip	equipment	team
3.	tomo:	I drink	I take	tome, volume
4.	trabajo:	I work	job	term paper

C. *¿Qué quieren Uds. que hagan estas personas?* Using the following list of phrases, answer the questions you hear on tape. You and a friend will be telling what you want a series of people to do for both of you. You will hear each question twice. First, listen to the list.

servirnos la comida   no poner la radio a las 11:00 P.M.
mandarnos los contratos   llamar a la doctora
darnos un aumento   decirnos el precio del grabador de vídeo

    MODELO: (¿Qué quieren Uds. que haga el enfermero? [*nurse*]) →
            <u>Queremos que llame a la doctora</u>.

1. ...   2. ...   3. ...   4. ...

D. *¡Vamos de vacaciones! Pero... ¿adónde?* The members of the Soto family can't decide where to go for their vacation. Tell what each person likes, using the oral and written cues.

    MODELO: ir a la playa (mi madre / nadar) →
            <u>A mi madre le gusta nadar. Le gustaría ir a la playa</u>.

1. ir a la playa   3. viajar a Europa
2. ir a las montañas   4. estar en casa todo el verano

E. *Dictado.* You will hear a conversation between a tourist who is interested in traveling to Cancún and a travel agent. Listen carefully and write down the requested information. First, listen to the list of information that is being requested.

el tipo de boleto que el turista quiere: _____

la fecha de salida: _____

la fecha de regreso (*return*):_____

la sección y la clase en que va a viajar: _____

la ciudad de la cual (*from which*) va a salir el avión:_____

el tipo de hotel que quiere: _____

el nombre del hotel en que se va a quedar: _____

F. *En la agencia de viajes.* Now you will participate in a similar conversation, partially printed in your manual, about making travel reservations. Complete it based on the cues suggested. You will hear a possible answer on the tape.

Here are the cues for your conversation.

> querer / 1 boleto de ida y vuelta / Miami
> April 18 / May 4
> ponerme: Ud. / fumar
> ya tener / reservaciones

—Buenos días. ¿En qué puedo servirle?

—Buenos días. _____

—¿Y las fechas de salida y regreso?

—Quiero salir _____ y regresar _____.

—Muy bien. ¿Prefiere la sección de fumar o la de no fuma?

—_____ , por favor.

—Cómo no. ¿Necesita Hotel?

—Gracias, pero _____

—Muy bien. Aquí tiene su boleto. ¡Buen viaje!

G. *En el restaurante La Valenciana.* You are eating lunch, the main meal of the day, in a Spanish restaurant in Madrid. Use the menu below to answer the waiter's questions. You will hear a possible answer on the tape. First, listen to the items on the menu.

Entremeses:

Jamón serrano
Champiñones al ajillo (mushrooms sautéed in garlic)
Calamares fritos (fried squid)

Entradas:

Gazpacho andaluz (cold tomato soup served with condiments)
Ensalada mixta (mixed green salad)
Alcachofas salteadas con jamón (artichokes sautéed with ham)

Platos fuertes:

Solomillo a la parrilla (beef cooked over a grill)
Paella valenciana (rice dish with seafood, chicken, pork, & saffron)
Cordero al chilindrón (lamb and red pepper stew)

Postres: ## Bebidas:

Flan de naranja (orange flan)   *Jerez (sherry)*   *Vino tinto*
Tarta de manzana (apple tart)   *Té*   *Vino blanco*
Peras al vino (pears in wine)   *Café*   *Agua mineral*

H. *Entrevista.* You will hear a series of questions. Each will be said twice. Answer based on your own experience. No answers will be given on the tape. (If you prefer, stop the tape and write the answer.)

Hablando de los bienes personales:

1. _____

2. _____

Hablando de las vacaciones:

3. _____

4. _____

Hablando de gustos y preferencias:

5. _____

6. _____

CAPÍTULO

13

Vocabulario: Los cuartos, los muebles y las otras partes de una casa

A. *¿Dónde están?* You will hear a series of conversations or parts of conversations. Write the number of the conversation next to the location in which it might be taking place. Don't be distracted by unfamiliar vocabulary or structures. Focus on what you *do* understand. First, listen to the list of locations.

___ una alcoba   ___ un comedor

___ una sala   ___ un cuarto de baño

___ una cocina

B. *¿Qué hay en esta sala?* You will hear the names of a series of items. Say the number to which each corresponds; then repeat the name. Follow the model.

MODELO: (una mesa) → El número seis es una mesa.

1. ...   2. ...   3. ...   4. ...   5. ...

C. *Entrevista: Hablando de casas ideales.* Imagine that you have the chance to design your own home. Answer the following questions about the features you would include. Each question will be said twice. You will hear a possible answer on the tape. (If you prefer, stop the tape and write the answer.)

1. _____

2. _____

3. _____

4. _____

Pronunciación y ortografía: Review of Linking

A. Pronounce the following phrases and sentences as if they were one word.

1. el escritorio   el hijo   el elefante   el otoño
2. los errores   los hoteles   las azafatas   las ideas
3. con Eduardo   son interesantes   en Alemania
4. de usted   para ella   la invitación   mi abuelo
5. mi hijo   me escuchan   la alfombra   lo oigo   entre ellos
6. ¿Qué es esto?
   Tienen un hijo y una hija.
   Aquí hay ocho estantes.
   Tienen un acuario en el estante.

B. *Dictado.* You will hear four sentences. Each will be said twice. Listen carefully and write what you hear.

1. _____
2. _____
3. _____
4. _____

Estructuras

26. Expressing Direct and Indirect Objects Together: Double Object Pronouns

A. *En casa, durante la cena.* Your brother is still hungry and asks about the different foods that might be left. Listen carefully and circle the items to which he is referring.

MODELO: (¿Hay más? Me la pasas, por favor.)
la sopa   el pan   el pescado

1. las galletas   la fruta   el helado
2. la carne   el postre   los camarones
3. la leche   el vino   las arvejas
4. las papas fritas   la cerveza   el pastel

You should have circled **el helado, los camarones, la leche,** and **las papas fritas.**

B. *En el restaurante El Charro.* You will hear a series of questions. Each will be said twice. Answer each based on the drawings. Use double object pronouns in your answers. You will hear a possible answer on the tape.

1. ...   2. ...   3. ...   4. ...

C. *¿Dónde está...?* Your roommate Carolina would like to borrow some things from you. Tell her to whom you gave each item, using double object pronouns and the written cues. You will hear each of Carolina's questions twice. Note: **di** means *I gave*.

> MODELO: (Oye, ¿dónde está tu diccionario?) Nicolás / necesitarlo para un examen →
> <u>Se lo di a Nicolás. Él lo necesita para un examen.</u>

1. Teresa / tener que estudiar el vocabulario
2. Juan / salir para México mañana
3. Nina / ir a una fiesta el sábado
4. Verónica / tener una cena elegante con su novio esta noche

Vocabulario: ¿Dónde vive Ud.? ¿Dónde quiere vivir?

A. *Definiciones.* You will hear a series of statements. Each will be said twice. Circle the letter of the word that is best defined by each.

1. a) el vecino   b) la dirección   c) la vista
2. a) los impuestos   b) el inquilino   c) el alquiler
3. a) la planta baja   b) las afueras   c) el centro
4. a) la vista   b) la luz   c) el gas
5. a) la portera   b) la dirección   c) el piso

B. *Entrevista: Hablando de la vivienda* (housing). You will hear a series of questions. Each will be said twice. Answer based on your own experience. No answers will be given on the tape. (If you prefer, stop the tape and write the answer.)

1. _____

2. _____

3. _____

4. _____

5. _____

Estructuras

27. Talking About the Past (1): Preterite of Regular Verbs and of **dar, hacer, ir,** and **ser**

A. *Minidialogo: Un problema con la agencia de empleos.* You will hear a dialogue followed by a series of statements. Circle the letter of the person who might have made each statement.

1. a) el ama de casa   b) el empleado de la agencia   c) la criada
2. a) el ama de casa   b) el empleado de la agencia   c) la criada
3. a) el ama de casa   b) el empleado de la agencia   c) la criada
4. a) el ama de casa   b) el empleado de la agencia   c) la criada

B. *¿Presente o pretérito?* You will hear a series of conversations or parts of conversations. Listen carefully and determine if the people are talking about the past or the present. Don't be distracted by unfamiliar vocabulary.

1. a) presente   b) pretérito
2. a) presente   b) pretérito
3. a) presente   b) pretérito
4. a) presente   b) pretérito
5. a) presente   b) pretérito

C. *¿Qué pasó ayer?* Practice telling what the following people did yesterday, using the oral and written cues.

Antes de la fiesta.

1. yo   2. mi compañero   3. nosotros

Antes del examen de química

4. Nati y yo   5. Diana   6. todos

D. *El viaje de los Sres. Blanco.* You will hear a series of questions about Mr. and Ms. Blanco's recent plane trip to Lima, Peru. Answer using the written cues.

1. 10:50 A.M.   4. 11:00 P.M.
2. vecino, el Sr. Ortega   5. hotel
3. leer revistas

Un poco de todo

A. *En el periódico: Amoblamiento y decoración.* The following ad appeared in an Argentinian newspaper. Listen to the ad. Then, when you hear the corresponding number, find the Spanish equivalent of the following words and phrases. Repeat the words and phrases when you hear the correct answer.

H. AMBROSI PROD

En amoblamientos de cocina, para nosotros contado son 50 meses

Plan 2000 es el único plan que le da la seguridad de tener una cocina de lujo. Plan 2000 es el más ventajoso, porque con Plan 2000 compra a precio de contado y lo paga hasta en 50 meses.

Tenga su amoblamiento de cocina totalmente de madera maciza y a medida. Con triple lustre de poliuretano, que proteje la belleza natural de la madera. Por eso su mueble será fácil de limpiar.

Téngalo en cuenta porque…

No es plan de ahorro, es

Sin sorteo

Sin licitación

Fecha de entrega a su elección

Ajust. P. F.

AMOBLAMIENTO 2000 CATAMARCA S.A.

Abierto: Lunes a sábados de 9 a 20 hs.
Domingos y feriados de 10 a 20 hs.

1. furnishings
2. delivery date

3. polyurethane
4. natural beauty

B. *Estrategias:* Word Families. You have practiced recognizing words from context based on their position or function in a sentence and on their similarity to English words of the same meaning. The job of guessing the meaning of unfamiliar words is often made easier if that word shares a root with a word you already know. Here is an example. You are familiar with the verb **temer.** You could probably guess that **el temor** means *fear* (a noun) and that **temeroso** means *fearful* (an adjective) if you were to see these unfamiliar words in context. Your knowledge of word endings and of aspects of Spanish grammar also helps you make educated guesses in this case.

Dictado. In this exercise, you will hear a series of sentences that contain words that share roots with words you already know. Each will be said twice. After you hear each sentence, write the related words in the corresponding spaces. First, listen to the words.

1. practicar: _____

2. acuario: _____

3. almacén: _____   _____

4. pescado: _____   _____

C. *Y para terminar... El el periódico: Pisos y apartamentos.* The following housing ads appeared in a Spanish newspaper. Look at the descriptions of the apartments and decide which one you are most interested in. Then answer the questions you will hear. If the ad for the apartment you have chosen doesn't contain the information requested in the questions, say **No lo dice.** No answers will be given on the tape.

1. ...   2. ...   3. ...   4. ...   5. ...   6. ...

Un paso más: Situaciones

A. *En busca de un cuarto.* In the following conversation, you will hear a description of a place you might want to live. Read the conversation silently, along with the speakers.

—¿Qué te pasa? Pareces muy preocupado.

—Llevo dos semanas buscando cuarto y... ¡nada!

—¿Qué tipo de cuarto buscas?

—Pues... quiero un cuarto para mí solo, que sea grande. Además, necesito muchos estantes para poner libros y un armario bien grande. También me gusta que el cuarto tenga mucha luz y que sea tranquilo.

—¿Nada más?

—Además quiero que esté cerca de la universidad, que tenga garaje, con derecho a usar la cocina, con teléfono... y ¡claro!, que sea barato.

—Hombre, no pides mucho.... Pero no te preocupes. Ahora que me lo dices, creo que hay uno un el edificio donde vive Rosario. ¡No sé por qué no se me ocurrió antes! ¿Sabes dónde está?

—Creo que sí. La voy a llamar ahora mismo. Te lo agradezco, ¿eh?

B. *Conversación: En busca de vivienda* (housing). Now you will participate in a similar conversation, partially printed in your manual, about looking for an apartment. Complete it based on your own experience. No answers will be given on the tape. You may want to record your answers.

—Cuánto tiempo hace que buscas (*How long have you been looking for...*) un apartamento?

— _____

—Y ¿qué tipo de apartamento quieres?

—Bueno, prefiero un apartamento que _____ y que tenga _____ alcoba(s). También

quiero uno con _____. Pero lo que más me importa es que esté _____ de la

universidad.

—¡Buena suerte! Ya sabes que mientras más cerca estés de la universidad, más alto va a ser el alquiler.

CAPÍTULO
14

Vocabulario: Los aparatos domésticos

A. *Descripción: El apartamento de David y Raúl.* You will hear a series of statements about the following drawing. Each will be said twice. Circle *C* if the statement is true or *F* if it is false. First, look at the drawing.

1. C F   2. C F   3. C F   4. C F   5. C F

B. Now you will hear a series of questions. Answer based on the preceding drawing and your own experience. Each question will be said twice. You will hear a possible answer on the tape.

1. ...   2. ...   3. ...   4. ...

Vocabulario: Más verbos útiles

A. *Descripción: El sábado en casa de la familia Hernández.* Tell what the following family members are doing, using the oral cues. Base your answers on the drawings. You will hear a possible answer on the tape.

MODELO: (despertar) → <u>Los hijos despiertan a sus padres</u>.

1.

2.

3.

4.

5.

6.

B. *¿Para qué sirven estos aparatos domésticos?* Your young friend Joselito wants to know what various appliances do. Answer his questions, using phrases chosen from the following list. You will hear each of his questions twice. First, listen to the list.

lavar la ropa sucia
acondicionar el aire
cocinar la comida
congelar la carne

tostar (ue) el pan
lavar los platos sucios
secar la ropa mojada (*wet*)

    MODELO: (¿Para qué sirve el lavaplatos?) → <u>Lava los platos sucios</u>.

1. ...   2. ...   3. ...   4. ...   5. ...

Pronunciación y ortografía: Punctuation, Intonation, and Rhythm

Dictado. You will hear the following sentences. Each will be said twice. Listen carefully for intonation. Repeat what you hear; then punctuate each sentence.

1. Cuál es tu profesión   Te pagan bien
2. Tú no la conoces verdad
3. Prefiere Ud. que le sirva la comida en el patio
4. Qué ejercicio más fácil
5. No sé dónde viven pero sí sé su número de teléfono

Estructuras

28. Expressing -*self* / -*selves*: Reflexive Pronouns

A. *Minidiálogo: Un día típico.* You will hear a description of a typical day in the life of Alicia and Miguel. Then you will hear a series of statements about the description. Circle *C* if the statement is true or *F* if it is false. You will practice getting the main idea.

1. C F   2. C F   3. C F

B. *Hábitos y costumbres: Todos somos diferentes.* You will hear a series of statements and questions. Each will be said twice. Answer using the written cues.

   MODELO: (Me levanto a las seis y media. ¿Y José?) 7:00 → <u>Se levanta a las siete</u>.

1. noche   4. impermeable
2. después   5. tarde
3. sofá

C. *Escenas domésticas.* Miguelito is asking the maid a lot of questions today. You will hear each question twice. Take the part of the maid and answer his questions according to the written cues. Use object pronouns when possible. ¡OJO! Not all verbs will be reflexive.

   MODELO: (¿Tengo que levantarme ahora mismo?) Sí,... →
             <u>Sí, Miguelito, levántese ahora mismo.</u>

1. Sí,...   2. Sí,...   3. Sí,...   4. No,...   5. No,...

Vocabulario: Talking About Obligation

Entrevista: Los quehaceres domésticos. In this interview, you will practice talking about your obligations with respect to household chores. You will hear each question twice. Answer based on your own experience. No answers will be given on the tape. (If you prefer, stop the tape and write the answer.)

1. _____

2. _____

3. _____

4. _____

5. _____

Estructuras

29. Talking About the Past (2): Irregular Preterites; Stem-Changing Preterites

A. *Minidiálogo: Pronóstico de un nombre.* You will hear a dialogue followed by a series of statements. Circle *C* if the statement is true or *F* if it is false.

1. C F   2. C F   3. C F

B. *La fiesta de cumpleaños.* Tell what happened at the party, using the oral cues.

1. estar en casa de Mario
2. tener que limpiar la casa
3. venir con comida y regalos
4. no poder asistir
5. ¡estar estupenda!

C. *La fiesta de despedida de Carmen.* You will hear a brief description of a going-away party for Carmen, narrated by Carmen. Then you will hear a series of questions about the party. Answer them based on the written cues, choosing one verb from each pair.

1. **decidí / decidió** dejar su puesto
2. **organicé / organizaron** una fiesta
3. **empezó / empecé** a llorar
4. **me reí / se rieron** y **hablaron / hablé** hasta las cinco
5. **se sintió / me sentí** un poco triste

D. *Descripción: ¿Qué hizo Rodolfo hoy?* Tell what Rodolfo did today after you hear the corresponding number for each drawing. Use the verbs and phrases listed. You will hear a possible answer on the tape.

1. hacer / camas

2. lavar / ropa

3. poner / lavaplatos

4. ir / mercado

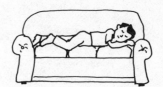

5. traer / comida a casa

6. dormir / toda la tarde

Un poco de todo

A. *Anuncios: Se venden aparatos domésticos.* You will hear a series of ads for appliances. Write the number of the ad next to the appliance described. First, listen to the list of appliances.

_____ un acondicionador aire

_____ una estufa

_____ un refrigerador

_____ una secadora

B. *Listening Passage.* You will hear a brief passage about architecture in the Hispanic world. Then you will hear a series of statements about the passage. Circle *C* if the statement is true or *F* if it is false.

1. C F   2. C F   3. C F   4. C F

C. *¿Qué hiciste ayer?* Using the preterite of the verbs below, tell what you did yesterday. Add any details you need, especially adverbs. No answers will be given on the tape. You may want to record your answers. First, listen to the list of verbs and phrases.

1. despertarse y levantarse a las...
2. apagar el despertador
3. bañarse y vestirse
4. tener tiempo para desayunar
5. llegar...

6. almorzar en...
7. trabajar hasta las...
8. regresar a casa
9. cenar
10. acostarse y dormirse

D. *Y para terminar... Descripción: En casa de los Delibes.* You will hear a series of statements about the following drawing. Each will be said twice. Circle *C* if the statement is true or *F* if it is false. First, look at the drawing.

1. C F   2. C F   3. C F   4. C F   5. C F   6. C F

CAPÍTULO

15

Vocabulario: Hablando de fiestas...

A. *Días festivos.* You will hear a series of dates. Each will be said twice. Circle the letter of the holiday that is usually celebrated on that date.

1. a) la Noche Vieja   b) la Nochebuena
2. a) el Día de los Muertos   b) el Día del Año Nuevo
3. a) la Navidad   b) la Pascua
4. a) el Día de los Muertos   b) la Noche Vieja
5. a) la Pascua Florida   b) el Día de Gracias

B. *Preguntas: ¿Qué hiciste la Navidad pasada?* You will hear a series of questions. Answer using the written cues. Use object pronouns when possible.

1. en casa
2. sí: venir todos mis tíos y primos
3. su novia
4. sí
5. debajo del árbol

C. *Descripción: Una fiesta de la Noche Vieja.* Describe how these people feel or what they are doing, by answering the questions you hear. Each will be said twice. You will hear a possible answer on the tape.

1. ...   2. ...   3. ...   4. ...   5. ...   6 ...

Pronunciación y ortografía: More on Stress and the Written Accent

A. Repeat the following words, paying close attention to stress and the written accent.

1. plato	azafata	trofeo	cocinan	interesantes
2. refrigerador	deber	legal	verdad	capital
3. doméstico	vólibol	máquina	líquido	vídeo
4. adiós	acción	vacación	avión	autobús

B. You have probably noticed that the written accent is an important factor in the spelling of some verb forms. It is also important for maintaining the original "sound" of a word to which syllables have been added.

When you hear the corresponding number, read the following pairs of words. Then repeat the correct pronunciation, imitating the speaker.

1. hablo / habló	5. joven / jóvenes	8. nación / naciones
2. pague / pagué	6. diga / dígame	9. francés / franceses
3. olvide / olvidé	7. haga / hágalo	
4. limpio / limpió		

C. *Dictado.* You will hear the following words. Each will be said twice. Write in an accent mark, if necessary.

1. jugo	5. sicologia	9. levantate
2. jugo	6. sicologo	10. levanta
3. describes	7. almacen	11. gusto
4. describemela	8. almacenes	12. gusto

Estructuras

30. Expressing *each other*: Reciprocal Actions with Reflexive Pronouns

Descripción: ¿Qué hacen estas personas? Using the written cues, tell what the following pairs of people are doing when you hear the corresponding number. You will be describing reciprocal actions. You will hear a possible answer on the tape.

1. quererse	3. darse la mano
2. escribirse	4. hablarse por teléfono.

Vocabulario: Más emociones

A. *Hablando de ambiciones y carreras.* You will hear three descriptions of people and their careers. Listen carefully and write the name of the person described next to the statement that best summarizes his or her achievements. In this exercise, you will practice listening for specific as well as general information.

_____ llegó a ser director(a) de la compañía.

_____ llegó a ser actor/actriz.

_____ se hizo millonario/a.

B. *¿Cómo reacciona Ud.?* Practice telling how you react to these situations, using the oral and written cues.

> MODELO: me olvido del cumpleaños de mi madre (ponerse avergonzado) →
> *Me pongo avergonzada cuando me olvido del cumpleaños de mi madre.*

1. mi novio habla con otras chicas
2. mis padres me quitan el coche
3. veo una película triste

4. hablo con mis profesores.
5. saco buenas notas

Estructuras

31. Descriptions and Habitual Actions in the Past: Imperfect of Regular and Irregular Verbs

A. *Minidiálogo: La nostalgia.* You will hear a dialogue followed by a series of statements about the dialogue. Circle *C* if the statement is true or *F* if it is false.

1. C F   2. C F   3. C F

B. *Describiendo el pasado: En la primaria.* Tell what you and others used to do in grade school, using the oral and written cues.

1. yo
2. Rodolfo
3. tú

4. todos
5. nosotros

C. *¿Qué hacían antes?* You will hear a series of sentences about present actions. Tell what used to happen, using the written cues.

> MODELO: (Ahora enseña química.) matemáticas → Antes enseñaba matemáticas.

1. California
2. muy mal
3. elegantemente

4. en clase turística
5. mucho

D. *Conversación: ¿Cómo era su niñez (childhood)?* You and a group of friends are having a conversation about your childhood. Answer their questions based on your own experience. Each question will be said twice. You will hear two possible answers for each question. Give your own answer, then listen to the possible answers. (If you prefer, stop the tape and write the answer.)

1. _____

2. _____

3. _____

4. _____

5. _____

Estructuras

32. Expressing Extremes: Superlatives

A. *Chismes* (Gossip) *de la boda de Julia y Patricio.* Your friend's wedding celebration has the best of everything. Answer some questions about it using the written cues.

> MODELO: (Son camisas elegantes, ¿verdad?) almacén →
> <u>Sí, son las camisas más elegantes del almacén</u>.

1. joyería (*jewelry store*)
2. fiesta
3. almacén
4. año
5. todos los invitados (*guests*)

B. *El mejor restaurante del mundo.* You will hear a series of questions about the "world's best restaurant." Answer using an emphatic form of the indicated adjective or adverb.

> MODELO: (¿Qué tal la ensalada?) sabroso → <u>Es sabrosísima</u>.

1. rico   2. bueno   3. caro   4. rápido

Un poco de todo

A. *Estrategias:* Recognizing Derivative Adjectives. You have already learned about the strategy of guessing words from context based on their roots and their endings. One group of endings can convert verbs into adjectives: **-ado** and **-ido**. You will learn how to use these endings in future chapters, but for now just concentrate on the meaning that they give to the word. For example, you can probably guess that **perdido** means *lost* (an adjective) and that **cerrado** means *closed* (also an adjective). Remember that adjectives that end in **-o** have four forms. In the following exercise, you will practice listening for adjectives derived from verbs you already know.

You will hear a series of unfamiliar adjectives. Each will be said twice. Write the number of each adjective next to the verb from which the adjective is derived.

comprar: _____   estudiar: _____

servir: _____   conocer: _____

contestar: _____   cocinar: _____

B. *Listening Passage.* You will hear a brief passage about Carnival celebrations in the Hispanic world. Then you will hear a series of statements about the passage. Circle *C* if the statement is true or *F* if it is false. The following words and phrases will appear in the listening passage. Listen to them before the passage is read.

> más conocidas (¿ / ?)
> temporada (*period of time*)
> la Cuaresma (*Lent*)
> los disfraces (*costumes, disguises*)
> vivos (*bright*)

1. C F   2. C F   3. C F   4. C F

C. *Y para terminar... Entrevista.* You will hear a series of questions about the last party you attended. Each will be said twice. Answer based on your own experience. No answers will be given on the tape. (If you wish, stop the tape and write your answer.)

1. _____
2. _____
3. _____
4. _____
5. _____
6. _____

Un paso más: Situaciones

A. *En una fiesta de Navidad.* You will hear a conversation about a Christmas party. Read it silently, along with the speakers.

A la llegada

—¡Chicos, cuánto gusto! ¡Felices Pascuas! Pasen, pasen.
—¡Hola, Antonieta! ¡Felices Pascuas!
—¿Por qué no vino Alejandro?
—Se me olvidó decirte que no pudo regresar. Perdió el vuelo de la tarde.
—Lo siento. Ahora pónganse cómodos y vamos a divertirnos. ¿Qué quieren tomar?
—Una bebida sin alcohol, por favor. Pero, primero, ¿dónde podemos dejar estas cosillas que trajimos?
—¡Ay, muchas gracias! ¡Muy amables! Pueden dejarlas en la cocina. Ahora bien: José Antonio preparó un ponche muy rico que a todos nos gusta.
—Oye, esta fiesta está estupenda. La música es fabulosa y ¡cuánta comida deliciosa!
—¡Pobre Alejandro! Se está perdiendo la mejor fiesta del año.

A la despedida

—Muchas gracias por venir.
—Gracias a ti. ¡Lo pasamos estupendamente!
—Y, como ya te dijimos, mañana vamos a estar aquí a las nueve para ayudarte a limpiar la casa.
—No es necesario que se molesten. Se lo agradezco, de verdad.
—No es molestia.
—Bueno, si insisten.... Seguro que entre todos vamos a terminar pronto.

B. Now you will hear another conversation about a holiday, partially printed in your manual. Then you will participate in a similar conversation. Complete it based on your own experience. No answers will be given on the tape.

—¿ _____

—Pues, en casa de unos amigos. Bailamos mucho y lo pasamos muy bien. ¿Y tú?

— _____

—¿Te divertiste?

— _____

CAPÍTULO

16

Vocabulario: Para estar en forma

A. *Algunas partes del cuerpo.* Identify the following body parts when you hear the corresponding number. Use **ser** and the appropriate form of the definite article.

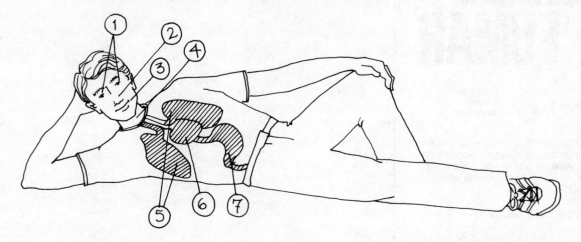

1. ...   2. ...   3. ...   4. ...   5. ...   6. ...   7. ...

B. *En el consultorio* (office) *de la doctora Vásquez: ¿Qué debo hacer para estar en buena salud?* You are a doctor whose patient wants to know what he should do to be in good health. Tell him what to do or what *not* to do, using the oral cues. Use formal commands, as in the model.

   MODELO: practicar algún deporte → <u>Practique Ud. algún deporte</u>.

1. ...   2. ...   3. ...   4. ...   5. ...   6. ...

C. *En el periódico: La salud.* You will hear the following ads from Hispanic newspapers. Listen to them and circle the Spanish words or phrases that express the following. First, listen to the list.

Deje de fumar
1. killers
2. medical treatment
3. a drug

Reg. S.S.A. -KOINJ

DEJE DE FUMAR

Distraiga sólo
2 horas
de su tiempo.

Uno de los asesinos de su salud, puede ser eliminado. La nicotina no es nada más un vicio, es una droga. Tratamiento médico que combate tanto la adicción como el hábito.

Solicite una cita al 520-32-61.

Instituto Roit, S.A. de C.V.

Lentes de contacto
4. a replacement pair
5. immediate replacement
6. soft or flexible

LENTES DE CONTACTO

1 Par de Lentes de Contacto más
1 Par de Repuesto blandas o flexibles   ⏣ 249
Por lentes especiales, consultar.
Una ventaja única que le asegura
LA INMEDIATA REPOSICION POR PERDIDA O ROTURA.

Lentes de Contacto de Primera Calidad con GARANTIA TOTAL.

Atención personalizada, a cargo de técnicos muy experimentados en esta especialidad.

● Decídase a consultarnos y benefíciese.

Laboratorio SAIS
Av. Córdoba 2466 · Buenos Aires
961-1310, 2145 y 3633

SAIS

50 años a la vanguardia
en el dominio de esta
depurada técnica visual.
–Consulte a su médico–

Pronunciación y ortografía: More on Stress and the Written Accent

A. You have probably noticed that when a pair of words is written the same but has different meanings, one of the words is accented. This accent is called a *diacritical* accent.

Repeat the following words, paying close attention to the meaning of each.

1. mi (*my*) / mí (*me*)
2. tu (*your*) / tú (*you*)
3. el (*the*) / él (*he*)
4. si (*if*) / sí (*yes*)
5. se (*oneself*) / sé (*I know; be* - informal command)
6. de (*of, from*) / dé (*give* - formal command; *give* - present subjunctive)
7. te (*you, yourself*) / té (*tea*)
8. solo (*alone, sole* - adjective) / sólo (*only* - adverb)
9. que (*that, which*) / ¿qué? (*what?*)
10. este (*this*) / éste (*this one*)

B. *Dictado.* Listen to the following sentences and determine by context whether or not the meaning of the underlined words requires a written accent. Each sentence will be said twice.

1. Creo <u>que este</u> regalo es para <u>mi</u>.
2. Aquí <u>esta tu te</u>. ¿<u>Que</u> más quieres?
3. <u>El</u> dijo <u>que te</u> iba a llamar a los ocho.
4. <u>Si</u>, <u>mi</u> amigo <u>se</u> llama Antonio.

Estructuras

33. Narrating in the Past: Using the Preterite and Imperfect

A. *Minidiálogo: No es para tanto...* You will hear a dialogue followed by a series of statements about the dialogue. Circle *C* if the statement is true or *F* if it is false.

1. C F   2. C F   3. C F

B. *¿Un sábado típico?* You will hear a series of sentences that describe a series of events. Form new sentences, using the written cues. Begin each sentence with **El sábado pasado....**

MODELO: Todos los sábados, Carlos se despertaba a las siete.) ocho →
         <u>El sábado pasado, se despertó a las ocho.</u>

1. mercado
2. café
3. hermana
4. después de la cena
5. tarde

C. *Una decisión difícil.* You will hear the following sentences about Laura's decision to leave her home town. Change the italicized verbs to the preterite or imperfect, according to the oral cues. In this exercise, you will practice narrating in the past.

MODELO: *Vivimos* en un pequeño pueblo en las montañas. (de niños)→
De niños, vivíamos en un pequeño pueblo en las montañas.

1. Mi madre *trabaja* en una panadería (*bakery*).
2. Mi padre *trabaja* en una tienda de comestibles (*food store*).
3. *Vamos* a la ciudad y *compramos* cosas que no *podemos* encontrar en nuestro pueblo.
4. *Consigo* trabajo permanente en la ciudad y *decido* dejar mi pueblo para siempre.
5. *Empiezo* a tomar clases de noche en la universidad y *dejo* mi puesto permanente por uno de tiempo parcial.
6. Mis padres *están* tristes porque ya no *vivo* con ellos, pero ahora están contentos con mi decisión.

Now answer the questions you hear based on the preceding story. Each question will be said twice.

1. ...   2. ...   3. ...   4. ...

D. *Descripción.* Tell what the following people are doing when you hear the corresponding number. Follow the model. You will hear a possible answer on the tape.

MODELO: cocinar / mientras / poner → Luis cocinaba mientras Paula ponía la mesa.

1. leer / cuando / entrar

2. cantar/ mientras / tocar

3. comer / cuando / sonar

4. llorar / mientras / ponerle una inyección

E. *Otro aspecto del mundo del trabajo.* You will hear a dialogue between Tomás and Teresa, two friends who are discussing an aspect of the working world. Then you will hear a series of statements. Circle the number of the statement that best summarizes the dialogue.

1 2 3

Now, using the written cues, give a summary of the main points of the dialogue. Use the preterite or imperfect in the first three sentences, the present in the last three. Add any necessary words. You will hear a possible answer on the tape.

1. Tomás / cambiar de / puesto / recientemente
2. no / estar / muy contento / con / puesto
3. lo peor / de / puesto / ser / sueldo
4. para Tomás / lo más importante / ser / familia
5. en / nuevo / puesto / darle / más / días festivos
6. por eso / Tomás / estar / muy contento

Vocabulario: En el consultorio del médico

A. *Para completar.* You will hear a series of incomplete statements. Each will be said twice. Circle the letter of the word or phrase that best completes each statement.

1. a) ponerle una inyección   b) respirar bien
2. a) los ojos   b) el corazón
3. a) una tos   b) un jarabe
4. a) las pastillas verdes   b) esta receta para el antibiótico
5. a) frío   b) un resfriado
6. a) saque la lengua   b) me duelen los ojos

B. *Entrevista: Hablando de la salud y el bienestar físico.* You will hear a series of questions. Each will be said twice. Answer based on your own experience. You will hear a possible answer on the tape. (If you prefer, stop the tape and write the answer.)

1. _____
2. _____
3. _____
4. _____
5. _____

Un poco de todo

A. *¿Cómo se sentía Reinaldo?* You will hear a brief description of how Reinaldo felt last week when he had the flu. Then you will hear the following statements, based on the description, that are out of sequence. Put them in correct sequence, using the numbers 1-5. The first one is done for you.

____ Por fin fue al médico.

____ Esta semana se siente mejor.

__1__ El lunes, Reinaldo se despertó con fiebre y dolor de cabeza.

____ En el consultorio del médico, éste le dio una receta para un antibiótico.

____ El martes, se sentía peor; le dolía el cuerpo entero.

B. *Dictado: ¿Cómo se sentía Reinaldo la semana pasada?* You will hear the description of Reinaldo's illness again. It will be said only once. Listen carefully and write the missing words.

Estuve _____ [1] _____ [2] la semana pasada. El lunes, cuando me desperté,

_____ [3] _____ [4] y _____ [5] _____ [6] la cabeza. También estaba un

poco _____ [7] y no podía _____ [8] bien. El martes _____ [9] a

_____, [10] pero _____ [11] _____ [12] fue que me dolía _____ [13] el

_____. [14] Por fin _____ [15] una cita con el _____ [16] para el miércoles y él

_____ [17] _____ [18] un _____. [19] Desafortunadamente, _____ [20] que

_____ [21] _____ [22] por tres días y _____ [23] al trabajo el resto de la

_____.[24] Como no tenía apetito, no _____ [25] _____ [26] y perdí tres o cuatro

libras. _____[27] semana, gracias a Dios, _____ [28] _____ [29] _____.[30]

¡Espero que no me vuelva a _____[31] este año!

C. *Listening Passage.* You will hear a brief passage about traditional or folk medicine. Then you will hear a series of statements about the passage. Circle *C* if the statement is true or *F* if it is false.

1. C F   2. C F   3. C F   4. C F

D. *Descripción.* The captions for the following cartoon will be read on the tape. Listen carefully; then answer the questions about the cartoon. You will hear a possible answer on the tape. First, listen to the following expressions that appear in the cartoon.

levantado (*up, out of bed*)
me he sacado de encima (*I got rid of*)
gripe (*flu*)

1. ...   2. ...   3. ...   4. ...   5. ...   6. ...

E. *Y para terminar... Entrevista: Preguntas personales.* You will hear a series of questions about what you used to do or did as a child. Each will be said twice. Answer based on your own experience. No answers will be given on the tape. (If you prefer, stop the tape and write the answer.)

1. _____

2. _____

3. _____

4. _____

5. _____

6. _____

7. _____

8. _____

REPASO

4

A. *Descripción: En casa de la familia Ruiz.* You will hear a series of statements about the following drawing. Circle *C* if the statement is true or *F* if it is false. Then you will be asked to describe some of the actions in the drawing. First, look at the drawing.

¿Cierto o falso?

1. C F   2. C F   3. C F   4. C F

Descripción

1. ...   2. ...   3. ...   4. ...

B. *Estrategias Repaso:* Getting the Main Idea. You will hear a brief article from a Spanish magazine. Then you will hear two statements. Circle the number of the statement that best summarizes the article.

1 2

C. *Estrategias: Repaso:* Predicting Content. The title of the ad in the activity is "¡A su salud! En Uruguay, el único centro termal marino de América del Sur." Jot down three pieces of information you expect to find in this ad, based on the title. You may write in English.

1. _____

2. _____

3. _____

Now you will hear the ad followed by a series of statements. Circle *C* if the statement is true or *F* if it is false. As you listen to the ad, check to see whether your predictions about content were correct.

1. C F   2. C F   3. C F   4. C F

¡A SU SALUD! En Uruguay, el único centro termal marino de América del Sur.

Podemos brindar a su salud con el más atractivo plan de turismo. Un turismo de salud, porque tenemos para usted: • 350 habitaciones con baño privado • Calefacción • Piscinas con agua termal marina a 38° y 34°, con hidromasaje • Comidas a tenedor libre • Casino con slots, ruleta, punto y banca, black jack • Confitería bailable con orquesta. EXTRAS: • Salas de sauna finlandés • Cama solar austríaca • Baños con agua de mar hipertermales con extracto de algas y burbujas • 3 canchas de tenis • Canchas de golf (Club del Lago). ¿Cómo lo llamaría usted? ¿Curarse en vacaciones... o divertirse curándose? Llámelo como quiera, pero conózcalo y... ¡salud!

D. *Hablando con el corredor de casas* (real-estate agent). You are a real-estate agent, and your clients, Mr. and Mrs. Calvo, have some questions about a house that you are going to show them this afternoon. Each question will be said twice. Answer their questions based on the following floor plan. Note: The word **mide** means *measures*. You will hear a possible answer on the tape.

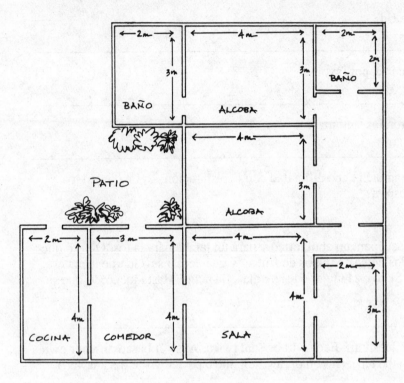

1. ...   2. ...   3. ...   4. ...   5. ...

E. *En busca de vivienda* (housing). You will hear three housing ads. Then you will hear descriptions of people who are looking for housing. Choose the house or apartment that best suits the needs of each person. You may want to jot down notes about the ads and the people in the spaces provided.

Anuncios   Personas

Anuncio 1:   1. los Sres. Robles
Anuncio 2:   2. Maricela y Ricardo
Anuncio 3:   3. Rogelio

F. *En la fiesta del Año Nuevo.* When you hear the corresponding number, describe what happened at your friend Mateo's New Year's Eve party. Use the following groups of words in the order given, and add any necessary words. ¡OJO! You will be using preterite and imperfect verb forms.

1. todos / llegar / nueve
2. Lisbet / traer / entremeses / vino
3. Rafael y yo / venir tarde / porque / perder / dirección / Mateo
4. Mateo / estar / contentísimo / porque / venir / su novia
5. todos / bailar / mientras / Tito / poner / discos
6. ser / tres / cuando / por fin / terminar / fiesta

G. *Conversación: En el consultorio de la doctora Rubio.* You have been feeling ill for three days. You have a fever and a cough and you feel nauseous. Using these symptoms and any other logical ones, complete the following conversation with Dr. Rubio. No answers will be given on the tape. First, listen to the conversation.

DRA. RUBIO: Buenas tardes. Pase Ud.

UD.:   _____

DRA. RUBIO: Dígame lo que le ocurre, por favor.

UD.:   _____

DRA. RUBIO: ¿Y cuándo empezaron los síntomas?

UD.:   _____

DRA. RUBIO: Bueno, parece que también tiene dificultad con la respiración.... ¿Le duelen los pulmones cuando respira?

UD.:   _____

DRA. RUBIO: Le voy a dar una receta para un antibiótico y para un jarabe para la tos. Quiero que tome muchos líquidos: agua, té, jugos de fruta... y que descanse. Guarde cama el resto de la semana. Si no está mejor en siete días, llámeme. Hasta luego, y ¡que se mejore pronto!

UD: _____

H. *Entrevista.* You will hear a series of questions. Each will be said twice. Answer based on your own experience. No answers will be given on the tape. (If you prefer, stop the tape and write the answer.)

Hablando de vacaciones

1. _____

2. _____

3. _____

Hablando de días festivos

4. _____

5. _____

6. _____

Hablando de la salud

7. _____

8. _____

9. _____

Vocabulario: Me levanté con el pie izquierdo

A. *Descripción: ¡Qué día más terrible!* You will hear a series of sentences. Each will be said twice. Write the letter of each sentence next to the appropriate drawing.

1.  —

2.  —

3.  —

4.  —

5.  —

B. *Presiones del trabajo.* You have been under a lot of pressure at work and it is affecting your judgment as well as other aspects of your life. Describe what has happened to you, using the oral cues.

MODELO: (no pagar mis cuentas) → <u>No pagué mis cuentas</u>.

1. ...   2. ...   3. ...   4. ...   5. ...   6. ...

C. *Reacciones:* You will hear a series of situations. React to each, choosing a sentence from the list. First, listen to the list.

Oye, ¿me puedes prestar tu coche?
Perdóneme. ¡Fue sin querer!
Profesor, tengo una pregunta.
Me imagino que te duelen las piernas.
¡Qué mala suerte!
Un frasco (*bottle*) de aspirinas, por favor.

> MODELO: (A Ud. le duele la cabeza y va a la farmacia. ¿Qué dice Ud.?) →
> <u>Un frasco de aspirinas, por favor.</u>

1. ...   2. ...   3. ...   4. ...   5. ...

Pronunciación y ortografía: Cognate Practice

A. Repeat the following words, paying close attention to the differences in spelling between the word and its English cognate.

1. correcto	5. teléfono	9. alianza
2. teoría	6. anual	10. físico
3. arcángel	7. clasificar	11. patético
4. químico	8. afirmar	12. ateísmo

B. *Dictado.* You will hear the following words. Each will be said twice. Listen carefully and write the missing letters.

1. _____ os _____ ato

2. a _____ en _____ ión

3. a _____ onfaco

4. _____ eología

5. o _____ osición

6. _____ otogra _____ ía

7. co _____ e _____ ión

8. ar _____ itecto

Nombre_____ Fecha _____ Clase_____

Estructuras

34. ¿Qué estás haciendo? Progressive Forms: **estar + -ndo**

A. *El sábado por la tarde: ¿Qué están haciendo estas personas?* Tell what the following people are doing when you hear the corresponding number and the oral cue.

1.

2.

3.

4.

5.

6.

B. *Descripción: ¿Qué están haciendo en este momento?* Using the present progressive of the following verbs, tell what each person in the Hernández family is doing at the moment. You will hear a possible answer on the tape. First, listen to the list of verbs.

ponerse   afeitarse   levantarse
vestirse   dormir   bañarse

MODELO: (1) → El bebé está durmiendo.

Capítulo 17   **141**

Vocabulario: Talking About How Things Are Done: Adverbs

Una reunión en Barcelona. Answer the following questions about your business trip to Barcelona, using the oral and written cues.

> MODELO: (¿Cuándo salió Ud. para el aeropuerto?) puntual / a las diez →
> <u>Salí puntualmente, a las diez</u>.

1. paciente
2. directo

3. inmediato
4. perfecto

5. muy bien

Estructuras

35. Expressing Unplanned or Unexpected Events: Another Use of **se**

A. *Dictado.* You will hear the following sentences. Each will be said twice. Listen carefully and write the missing words.

1. A ellos _____ _____ _____ el número de teléfono de Marta.

2. A Juan _____ _____ _____ los anteojos.

3. No quiero que _____ _____ _____el equipaje en el aeropuerto.

4. A los niños _____ _____ _____ los juguetes.

B. *¡Qué distraídos estuvimos ayer!* Tell how distracted you were yesterday, using the oral and written cues. You will begin each sentence with **Se me...**

1. olvidar / sacar la basura
2. olvidar / poner el despertador
3. romper / muchos platos
4. quedar / el dinero en casa
5. caer / los vasos

C. *Descripción: ¿Qué pasó el fin de semana pasado?* You and your friends gave an unsuccessful birthday party. When you hear each name, tell what happened based on the drawing, using **se**. First, look at the drawing.

1. ...   3. ...   5. ...

2. ...   4. ...

Un poco de todo

A. *Situaciones delicadas.* You will hear three situations. Choose the best solution or reaction to each.

1. a) ¡Ay, me hice daño en la mano!
   b) ¡Qué mala suerte, Sr. Ramos! ¿Tiene otro vaso?
   c) Lo siento muchísimo, Sr. Ramos. Fue sin querer. ¿Puedo comprarle otro?
2. a) No me importa que no te guste el menú. Vamos a comer aquí de todas formas (*anyway*).
   b) Lo siento mucho, pero pensé que te gustaría este restaurante. ¿Quieres ir a otro?
   c) Bueno, yo me quedo aquí, pero si tú quieres irte, a mí no me importa.
3. a) No se preocupe. Estoy bien.
   b) Mire, señor, si sus niños no dejan de hacer tanto ruido, voy a llamar a la policía.
   c) Por favor, señor, dígale a sus niños que no hagan tanto ruido... ¡Tengo un dolor de cabeza tremendo!

B. *Estrategias: More on Listening for General and Specific Information.* As you know, it helps to know what you are listening to *before* you listen. In the following exercise, you will practice this strategy by listening to the true/false statements before the article is read.

En el periódico: Gente. You will hear a brief article that appeared in a Spanish newspaper. Then you will hear a series of statements about the article. Circle *C* if the statement is true or *F* if it is false.

1. C F   2. C F   3. C F   4. C F

C. *Y para terminar... Entrevista.* You will hear a series of questions. Each will be said twice. Answer based on your own experience. No answers will be given on the tape. (If you prefer, stop the tape and write the answer.)

1. _____
2. _____
3. _____
4. _____
5. _____

Un paso más: Situaciones

A. *Incidentes de la vida diaria.* You will hear the following brief dialogues that illustrate how to act politely in Spanish in different situations. Read the dialogues silently, along with the speakers.

En una mesa o dondequiera que sea

—¡Oh! Discúlpeme. ¡Qué torpeza! Permítame que le limpie la camisa.
—No se preocupe. No es nada.
—Lo siento muchísimo.

En el autobús o en el metro

—Sígueme. Hay un sitio en el fondo.
—¡Hombre! Es imposible llegar allí.
—¿Tú crees? Mira.... Con permiso.... disculpe, señora, fue sin querer.... Con permiso.... Perdone.... Permiso, gracias.... ¡Huy! Perdón, lo siento, señora.
—¡Mal educado!

Al llegar tarde a una cita

—¡Uf! Lo siento. Créeme que no era mi intención llegar tan tarde. De verdad. Fue culpa del auto.
—Anda .... No te voy a regañar por diez minutos de retraso. No importa.

Al olvidar algo

—Oye, ¿trajiste los apuntes que te pedí?
—¿Los apuntes? ¿Qué apuntes? ¡Ay! Si ya decía yo que se me olvidaba algo. Se me ha pasado por completo. Lo lamento. Te los llevo el lunes, sin falla.
—Bueno, bueno... . No es para tanto.

B. Now you will participate in two conversations, partially printed in your manual. Use expressions from the list below or any others that are appropriate. You will hear a possible answer on the tape. First, listen to the list.

perdón	no se preocupe
¡lo siento!	no te preocupes
fue sin querer	está bien

1. En la farmacia: Ud. se da con una señora y a ella se la cae el frasco (*jar*) de medicina que llevaba.

    SRA.:   ¡Ay, no!... ¡el frasco!

    UD.:   _____

    SRA.:   ¿Qué voy a hacer? Esa medicina era para mi hijito, que está enfermo.

    UD.:   _____. Yo le compro otro frasco.

2. En el aeropuerto: Ud. se equivoca y toma el asiento de otra persona. Cuando ésta vuelve, quiere que Ud. le dé su puesto.

    SR.:   Perdón, pero ése es mi asiento.

    UD.:   _____. Aquí lo tiene.

    SR.:   Muchas gracias.

CAPÍTULO
18

Vocabulario: En la estación de gasolina

A. *Definiciones: Hablando de coches.* You will hear a series of statements. Each will be said twice. Circle the letter of the word that is best defined by each.

1. a) la batería   b) la gasolina   4. a) la esquina   b) la carretera
2. a) la licencia   b) el camino   5. a) el accidente   b) el taller
3. a) el semáforo   b) los frenos

B. *Identificaciones.* Identify the following items when you hear the corresponding number. Begin each sentence with **Es un...** , **Es una...** , or **Son....**

C. *Descripción.* Answer the questions you hear, based on the preceding drawing. Each question will be said twice. You will hear a possible answer on the tape.

1. ...   2. ...   3. ...   4. ...   5. ...   6. ...

D. *En el periódico: Venta de autos.* The following ads appeared in an Argentinian newspaper. Scan them and decide which car you want to buy. Then you will hear a series of questions. Each will be said twice. Answer them according to the ad you chose. No answers will be given on the tape. If the information requested in the question is not in the ad, answer with **No lo dice.**

```
★ M.BENZ 280 CE 1978
Verde, tapizado crema, impec
aire acond, direc hidr antena
     eléctrica u$s 16.500
    AUTOMOTRICES
    ALEMANAS S.R.L.
  Av. de Los Incas 5023/29 Cap
```

```
  RENAULT 18 GTX 84
Una unidad excepcional Para
llevárselo y lucirlo Pocos Km y
   buen uso Acepto ptas fac
   CORRIENTES 4242
       CAPITAL
```

1. ...   2. ...   3. ...   4. ...

Pronunciación y ortografía: More Cognate Practice

A. *False Cognates.* Unlike true cognates, false cognates do not have the same meaning in English as they do in Spanish. Repeat the following words, some of which you have already seen and used actively, paying close attention to their pronunciation and true meaning in Spanish.

la carta (*letter*)
dime (*tell me*)
emocionante (*thrilling*)
asistir (*to attend*)
el pan (*bread*)

el éxito (*success*)
sin (*without*)
el pie (*foot*)
actual (*current, present-day*)
actualmente (*nowadays*)

embarazada (*pregnant*)
el pariente (*relative*)
dice (*he/she says*)
la red (*net*)

B. You will hear the following paragraph from an article in a Spanish newspaper. Pay close attention to the pronunciation of the indicated cognates. Then you will practice reading the paragraph. You may want to record your reading.

El *ministro de Transportes y Comunicaciones*, Abel Caballero, ha *declarado* que el Gobierno está dando los primeros pasos para la *construcción* de *un satélite* español de *telecomunicaciones* que, de tomarse la *decisión final*, *comenzará* a ser *operativo* en 1992. (...)
 Muchos de los *componentes* del *satélite* tendrían que ser *importados*, pero al menos el treinta y seis por ciento los podría construir la *industria* española.

Estructuras

36. Expressing Uncertainty: Use of the Subjunctive in Noun Clauses: Doubt and Denial

A. *Comentarios sobre un coche.* You will hear a series of statements about the drawing. Circle *C* if the statement is true or *F* if it is false.

1. C   F
2. C   F
3. C   F

B. *¿Indicativo o subjuntivo?* You will hear a series of sentences. Each will be said twice. Tell whether the sentence expresses certainty (indicative) or doubt (subjunctive).

1. a) certainty   b) doubt   3. a) certainty   b) doubt
2. a) certainty   b) doubt   4. a) certainty   b) doubt

C. *¡Mi coche no funciona!* Practice telling what you should do when your car doesn't work well, using the oral and written cues.

    MODELO: Llevo el auto al taller. (Es posible que) → <u>Es posible que lleve el auto al taller</u>.

1. Es un auto viejo, pero...
2. El mecánico lo puede arreglar.
3. Sí, pero te cobran (*they'll charge*) mucho.
4. Bueno, puedo manejarlo así, en estas condiciones.
5. Y los frenos funcionan perfectamente.
6. Tienes razón. No debes manejarlo así.

D. *¿Qué piensa Ud.?* Your friend Josefina has made a series of statements. You will hear each one twice. Respond to each, using the written cues.

    MODELO: (Juan trae los contratos.) No creo... → <u>No creo que Juan traiga los contratos</u>.

1. No creo...   3. Dudo...   5. ¡Qué lástima... !
2. Es verdad...   4. Es increíble...   6. No dudo...

E. *De viaje.* Your friend Antonio is very nervous about your upcoming plane trip and is continuously asking you questions. You will hear each question twice. Answer negatively, using object pronouns in your answers, when possible.

    MODELO: (¿Crees que Teresa va a perder los boletos?) → <u>No, no creo que los pierda</u>.

1. ...   2. ...   3. ...   4. ...

Vocabulario: Putting Things in Rank Order: Ordinals

Descripción: ¿En qué piso... ? You will be asked to tell on what floor a number of families live or
businesses are located. Each question will be said twice. Answer based on the following drawing. First,
look at the drawing.

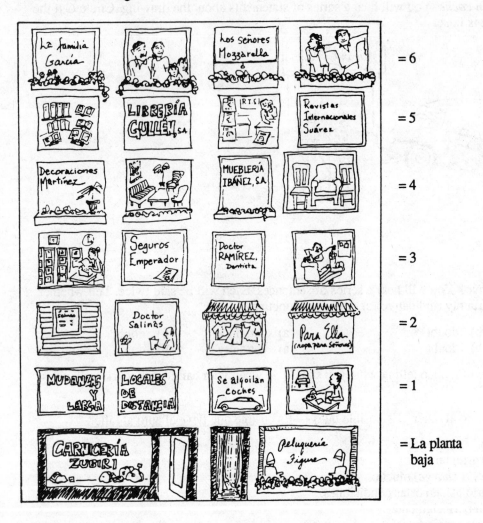

= 6

= 5

= 4

= 3

= 2

= 1

= La planta
baja

1. ...   2. ...   3. ...   4. ...   5. ...   6. ...   7. ...

Estructuras

37. Expressing Influence, Emotion, Doubt, and Denial: Uses of the Subjunctive in Noun Clauses: A Summary

A. *Minidiálogo: En el taller.* You will hear a dialogue followed by a series of statements. Circle the letter of the person who might have made each statement.

1. a) cliente   b) empleado   3. a) cliente   b) empleado
2. a) cliente   b) empleado   4. a) cliente   b) empleado

B. *Comprando coche.* Form new sentences, using the oral cues.

1. —¿Qué quiere Ud. que haga el vendedor? (enseñarme los últimos modelos) →
   —Quiero que me enseñe los últimos modelos.

   a. ...   b. ...   c. ...

2. —¿Qué es lo que le sorprende? (costar tanto los coche) →
   —Me sorprende que cuesten tanto los coches.

   a. ...   b. ...   c. ...

C. *Entrevista.* You will hear a series of questions about your opinions concerning the future. Each will be said twice. Answer based on your own experience. No answer will be given on the tape. (If you prefer, stop the tape and write the answer.)

1. _____

2. _____

3. _____

4. _____

5. _____

Un poco de todo

A. *En el extranjero: Se venden y se alquilan coches.* You will hear the following ad. Then you will hear a series of statements about the ad. Circle *C* if the statement is true or *F* if it is false. The following words appear in the ad.

cualquier (*any other*)
fábrica (*factory*)
aduana (*customs duty, fee*)
S.A. (Sociedad Anónima) (*Incorporated [Inc.]*)

1. C F   2. C F   3. C F   4. C F

B. *Listening Passage.* You will hear a brief passage about an industry in Latin America. Then you will hear a series of statements about the passage. Circle *C* if the statement is true or *F* if it is false.

1. C F   2. C F   3. C F   4. C F

C. *Y para terminar... Entrevista.* You will hear a series of questions. Each will be said twice. Answer based on your own experience. No answers will be given on the tape. (If you prefer, stop the tape and write the answer.)

1. _____

2. _____

3. _____

4. _____

5. _____

6. _____

CAPÍTULO
19

Vocabulario: Las computadoras / Los ordenadores

A. *Identificación.* Identify the following objects when you hear the corresponding number. Begin each sentence with the correct form of **ser** and the indefinite article, if needed.

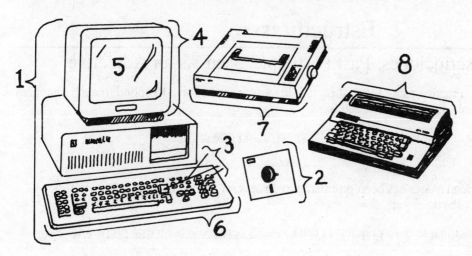

B. *Definiciones.* You will hear a series of statements. Each will be said twice. Choose the word that is best defined by each.

1. a) el inglés   b) el lenguaje
2. a) archivar   b) diseñar
3. a) la memoria b) los discos

4. a) el técnico (*technician*) b) el programador
5. a) la informática   b) la pantalla

C. *Diálogo: En la tienda de computadoras.* You will hear a conversation followed by a series of statements. Circle *C* if the statement is true or *F* if it is false. The following words appear in the conversation. Listen to them before the conversation is read.

escritos (*written*)
principiantes (*beginners*)
aplicaciones (*applications, uses*)

reparar (*to repair*)
hojas (*sheets [of paper]*)

1. C F   2. C F   3. C F   4. C F   5. C F

Pronunciación y ortografía: Nationalities

A. Repeat the following names of countries and the nationalities of those who were born there.

1. Nicaragua - nicaragüense
   el Canadá - canadiense
   los Estados Unidos - estadounidense
   Costa Rica - costarricense

2. la Argentina - argentino/a
   el Perú - peruano/a
   Colombia - colombiano/a
   Bolivia - boliviano/a

3. el Uruguay - uruguayo/a
   el Paraguay - paraguayo/a
4. Honduras - hondureño/a
   Panamá - panameño/a

el Brasil - brasileño/a
5. Guatemala - guatemalteco/a
   Portugal - portugués (portuguesa)
   Inglaterra - inglés (inglesa)

B. Now you will hear a series of nationalities. Each will be said twice. Repeat each and write the number of the nationality next to the country of origin. First, listen to the list of countries.

___ Chile

___ El Salvador

___ Puerto Rico

___ el Ecuador

___ Venezuela

___ Israel

Estructuras

38. Más descripciones: Past Participle Used As an Adjective

A. *Consecuencia lógicas.* Practice using the past participle to describe actions. Respond to each sentence you hear, telling the probable outcome of the action.

MODELO: (Escribí la composición.) → <u>Ahora la composición está escrita</u>.

1. ...   2. ...   3. ...   4. ...   5. ...

B. *¿Todavía no?* Your friend Marta has been promising to do several things for a long time, but she is a procrastinator. What hasn't she done yet?

MODELO: (Marta me dijo que iba a preparar la cena.) → <u>Sí, pero todavía no está preparada</u>.

1. ...   2. ...   3. ...   4. ...

Estructuras

40. ¿Qué has hecho? Present Perfect Indicative

A. *Minidiálogo: ¿Lo has leído ya?* You will hear a dialogue followed by a series of statements about the dialogue. Circle the letter of the person who might have made each statement, based on the dialogue. In this exercise, you will practice listening for the main idea.

1. a) Amalia   b) Rogelio
2. a) Amalia   b) Rogelio
3. a) Amalia   b) Rogelio

B. *En la oficina: ¿Qué han hecho estas personas esta mañana?* Practice telling what the following people have already done. Use the written and oral cues.

1. el secretario
2. la directora
3. tú

4. nosotros
5. todos

C. *¿Te puedo ayudar?* You have a lot to do before a dinner party, and your friend Ernesto wants to know if he can be of help. You appreciate his offer, but you have already done the things he asks about. You will hear each of his questions twice. Answer them according to the model.

MODELO: (¿Quieres que llame a los señores Moreno?) → <u>No, gracias, ya los he llamado</u>.

1. ...   2. ...   3. ...   4. ...   5. ...

D. *Entrevista.* You will hear a series of questions. Each will be said twice. Answer based on your own experience. No answers will be given on the tape. (If you prefer, stop the tape and write the answer.)

1. _____
2. _____
3. _____
4. _____
5. _____

Un poco de todo

A. *Descripción: Una familia de la era de la tecnología.* You will hear five brief descriptions. Write the letter of each description next to the drawing that it describes. ¡OJO! Not all the drawings will be described. First, look at the drawings.

1.  ____

2.  ____

3.  ____

4. 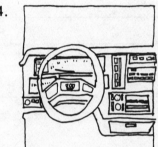 ____

5.  ____

6.  ____

B. *Estrategias: More Cognate Patterns.* In previous chapters you practiced identifying cognates by their endings or suffixes. Here are some additional cognate patterns.

comunismo	=	commun*ism*
turista	=	tour*ist*
lealtad	=	loyal*ty*
conjetura	=	conjec*ture*

You will hear a series of words. Listen carefully to them, paying particular attention to suffixes, and circle the letter of the English equivalent. ¡OJO! Some cognate patterns from previous chapters are included.

1. a) liberate   b) liberty
2. a) optimism   b) optimist
3. a) structure   b) structurally
4. a) reality   b) realist
5. a) romanticism   b) romantic

C. *El sábado por la mañana.* Roberto and Laura have many things to do today. Listen carefully and number their activities from 1 to 5. First, listen to the list of things they have to do.

___ llevar la impresora al taller   ___ pasar por la farmacia

___ ir al banco   ___ regresar a casa

___ salir a cenar fuera

D. *Y para terminar... Una canción.* The following song is popular among Spanish university students.

      Pim-pi-ri-rim-pim-pím

A mí me gusta el pim-pi-ri-rim-pim-pím
Con la botella empiná-pa-ra-ra-pa-pá.°   *tilted, raised*
Con el pim-pi-ri-rim-pim-pím,
Con el pa-pa-ra-ra-pa-pá.
Al que no le gusta el vino es un animal,
Es un animal...
...O no tiene un real.°   *coin (money)*

Un paso más: Situaciones

A. *Un servicio extraordinario.* You will hear the following dialogue that deals with technology. Read the dialogue silently, along with the speakers.

—Buenas. ¿Qué desea?
—Necesito que alguien me arregle esta impresora.
—Bien. Puede dejarla y pasar mañana o pasado mañana a recogerla.
—Pero... es que estoy haciendo un trabajo importante y ... quisiera tenerla pronto, si fuera posible.
—Bueno, si se trata de un caso de urgencia, de acuerdo. Llévela allí delante. Alguien la va a atender en seguida.
—Muchas gracias. Muy amable.

B. Now you will participate in a similar conversation, partially printed in your manual. Use expressions from the following list or any others that are appropriate. No answers will be given on the tape. You may want to record your answers. First, listen to the list.

el monitor
escribir un informe importantísimo
arreglármelo esta tarde
mil gracias

EMPLEADA: Buenas. ¿Qué desea?

UD.: Necesito que alguien me arregle _____.

EMPLEADA: No hay problema. Si no es algo serio, puede recogerlo en dos o tres días. Si es algo

complicado, es posible que tardemos una semana o más en arreglarlo.

UD.: Pero... es que estoy _____ y necesito que

_____, si es posible.

EMPLEADA: Bueno, si se trata de un caso de urgencia, se lo arreglamos inmediatamente.

UD.: _____.

CAPÍTULO

20

Vocabulario: ¿Cuál prefieres, la ciudad o el campo?

A. *¿La ciudad o el campo?* You will hear a series of statements. Each will be said twice. Circle the letter of the location you associate with each.

1. a) la ciudad   b) el campo   4. a) la ciudad   b) el campo
2. a) la ciudad   b) el campo   4. a) la ciudad   b) el campo
3. a) la ciudad   b) el campo   4. a) la ciudad   b) el campo

B. *En el campo.* Imagine that as a child you used to spend your summers in the country. Tell what you used to do, or how you used to feel, using the oral cues.

    MODELO: (madrugar todos los días) → <u>Madrugaba todos los días</u>.

1. ...   2. ...   3. ...   4. ...

C. *Gustos y preferencias.* You will hear descriptions of two people, Nicolás and Susana. Then you will hear a series of statements. Write the number of each statement next to the name of the person who might have made it.

Nicolás: _____

Susana: _____

Pronunciación y ortografía: Repaso

A. When you hear each number, read the corresponding Hispanic proverb; then listen to the correct pronunciation and repeat it.

1. Llamar al pan, pan y al vino, vino.
2. El agua para bañarse, el vino para beberse.
3. Quien mucho duerme, poco aprende.
4. No hay mal que por bien (*for a good reason*) no venga.
5. No hay regla sin excepción.
6. No hay montaña tan alta que un asno (*burro*) cargado de oro no la suba.

B. *Dictado.* You will hear a series of sentences. Each will be said twice. Listen carefully and write what you hear.

1. _____

2. _____

3. _____

4. _____

Estructuras

40. Dudo que lo hayas hecho: Present Perfect Subjunctive

A. *Minidiálogo: ¿Cambio de ritmo?* You will hear a dialogue followed by a series of statements. Circle the letter of the person who might have made each statement.

| 1. | a) Aurelia | b) Rafael | 3. | a) Aurelia | b) Rafael |
| 2. | a) Aurelia | b) Rafael | 4. | a) Aurelia | b) Rafael |

B. *Dudo que lo hayan hecho...* Your friends and family members are procrastinators, and you seriously doubt that they have done the things they said they would do. Use the oral and written cues to tell what you doubt.

> MODELO: Marta (hacer su tarea) → <u>Dudo que Marta haya hecho su tarea</u>.

1. Roberto
2. mis hermanitos
3. mis padres
4. tú
5. Elisabet

C. *Un caso de contaminación ambiental.* Imagine that a case of environmental pollution was discovered earlier this year in your community. Using the oral and written cues, form sentences that express what the residents have said about the incident. Follow the model.

> MODELO: ya estudiar el problema (es probable) →
> <u>Es probable que ya hayan estudiado el problema</u>.

1. todavía no avisar (*to notify*) a todos los habitantes de la ciudad
2. ya consultar con los expertos
3. descubrir la solución todavía
4. ya resolver el problema

Vocabulario: El medio ambiente

Un desacuerdo. You will hear a brief conversation between two friends, Arturo and Luciano, who disagree on certain environmental issues. Complete the following sentences, based on their conversation.

1. Según Arturo, las empresas _____ _____ (*contaminar*) el medio ambiente.

2. Luciano duda que las empresas (*corporations*) _____ _____ (*ser*) irresponsables.

3. Luciano cree que lo que _____ _____ (*decir*) Arturo no es totalmente cierto.

4. Arturo duda que las empresas _____ _____ (*empezar*) a resolver algunos de los problemas.

Estructuras

41. El infinitivo: Verb + Infinitive: Verb + Preposition + Infinitive

A. *Ventajas y desventajas de la era de la tecnología.* You will hear the following cartoon caption. Then you will hear a series of statements. Circle *C* if the statement is true or *F* if it is false. You will practice listening for specific as well as general information.

—*Yo quería ir a su oficina a pagar la tasa de estacionamiento,° pero no pude hacerlo porque no encontré sitio para estacionar.*

1. C F   2. C F   3. C F

B. *¿Qué hacen sus amigos?* Answer the question, using the oral and written cues.

MODELO: invitarme (salir con ellos) → <u>Me invitan a salir con ellos</u>.

1. ayudarme   2. invitarme   3. insistir   4. tratar

C. *Situaciones.* You will hear a series of situations. Answer using phrases from the list. ¡OJO! Not all phrases will be used. First, listen to the list.

explicarle lo que pasó   llevarlo al taller
limpiar el parabrisas   llamar al médico
ponerles cadenas (*chains*) a las llantas

1. ...   2. ...   3. ...   4. ...

Un poco de todo

A. *Conversación: Ventajas y desventajas.* You will hear a conversation, partially printed in your manual. Then you will participate in a similar conversation. Complete it based on your own experience. No answers will be given on the tape.

—¿Dónde estás más a gusto, en el campo o en la ciudad?

—Me encanta(n) _____

—¿Y qué te gusta hacer cuando estás allí?

— _____

—Pero también tiene sus inconvenientes, ¿no?

—¡ _____ !

B. *Listening Passage.* You will hear an article from a Hispanic magazine about **Motorola de México**. Then you will hear a series of statements about the article. Circle *C* if the statement is true of *F* if it is false.

1. C F   2. C F   3. C F   4. C F

C. *Entrevista.* You will hear a series of questions. Answer based on your own experience. No answer will be given on the tape. (If you prefer, stop the tape and write the answer.)

1. _____

2. _____

3. _____

4. _____

5. _____

D. *Y para terminar... Una canción.* "Triste estaba el Rey David" is a fifteenth-century Spanish song written by Alonso de Mudarra.

Triste estaba el Rey David

Triste estaba el Rey David,
Triste y con gran pasión,
Cuando le vinieron nuevas°   *news*
De la muerte de Absalón.°   *son of David*

Cuando le vinieron nuevas
De la muerte de Absalón,
Palabras triste° decía,   tristemente
Salidas del corazón.°   Salidas... Que venían del
                                                               corazón

REPASO

5

A. *Definiciones.* You will hear a series of definitions. Each will be said twice. Write the number of the definition next to the word that is best defined by each. First, listen to the list of words.

_____ puro   _____ la esquina

_____ el semáforo   _____ la programadora

_____ un hombre destraído   _____ la vivienda

B. *¿Dónde están estas personas?* You will hear a series of brief conversations or parts of conversations. Write the number of each next to the location in which the conversation might be taking place. First, listen to the list of locations.

_____ una gasolinera   _____ una tienda de computadoras

_____ una ciudad   _____ el campo

_____ un auto

C. *Estrategias: Repaso:* Recognizing Word Patterns. In this exercise you will practice listening for Spanish suffixes that have an English equivalent. You will hear a series of sentences containing words with suffixes you have seen in previous **Estrategias** sections. Some of the words are cognates; some are not. Each will be said twice. Circle the appropriate English equivalent based on context and the suffixes. Read the choices when you hear the corresponding number, *before* you hear each sentence.

MODELO: (Están *completamente* satisfechos.)
         a) complete   b) completely

1. a) atheism   b) atheist
2. a) parked   b) parking
3. a) developed   b) to develop
4. a) technical   b) technique
5. a) really   b) reality

D. *Un día típico.* You will hear a description of a day in Ángela's life, narrated in the past. Then you will hear a series of questions. Answer based on the description you hear. First, listen to the questions and try to get an idea of the information for which you need to listen.

1. ...   2. ...   3. ...   4. ...   5. ...

E. *¡Qué día más fatal! ¿Qué le pasó a Antonio?* Tell what happened to Antonio when you hear the corresponding number. Use preterite verb forms.

1. dormir muy mal anoche   5. quedársele en casa un reporte
2. despertarse a las cuatro de la mañana 6. tener que regresar a casa
3. no poder desayunar   7. llegar muy tarde al trabajo
4. perder el autobús   8. despedirlo su jefa

F. *Descripción.* Using the written cues, tell what the following people are doing when you hear their names. Use additional words to complete the meaning of each sentence. You will hear a possible answer on the tape.

MODELO: llenar (el mecánico) → <u>El mecánico está llenando las llantas de aire.</u>

1. estacionar

2. editar

3. mudarse

4. arreglar

5. construir

G. *En el periódico.* The following ad appeared in a Mexican newspaper. When you hear each number, give the Spanish equivalent of the corresponding word. First, look at the ad.

MEGACENTRO

Somos el número uno en COMPUTADORAS CORONA

CORONA PC-HD 20-14

— 512 KB Memoria Principal
— 1 Drive de 360 KB
— Disco Duro de 20 MB
— Monitor Monocromático
— MS DOS, GW BASIC, Tutoriales

$2.750,000.00 + IVA*

DENKI corona

Homero 408,
México, D. F.
250-32-55,
545-56-45

25 Poniente 1101,
Puebla, Pue.
(22) 43-77-28,
40-61-88

MEJOR VENTA DE LA SEMANA

Regulador Cobol 1/2 KVA $130,000.00
No Break Signal 8 + 150 Watts $290,000.00
Disco Duro 20 MB Interno $816,000.00
Diskettes Verbatim DSDD Caja 10 ....$ 23,000.00
Impresora Delta 15" de Ancho 180 CPS $860,000.00

DISTRIBUIDOR PREGUNTE POR SUS PRECIOS

* (Precio válido hasta el 21 de agosto)

1. hard disc
2. monochrome
3. tutorials

4. regulator
5. ... 6. ... 7. ...

H. *Entrevista: Temas diversos.* You will hear a series of questions. Each will be said twice. Answer based on your own experience. No answers will be given on the tape. (If you prefer, stop the tape and write the answer.)

1. _____

2. _____

3. _____

4. _____

5. _____

6. _____

7. _____

8. _____

CAPÍTULO
21

Vocabulario: Los pasatiempos

A. *Preguntas: Los ratos libres.* You will hear a series of questions about how you and others spent your free time in the past. Each will be said twice. Answer using cues chosen from the following list. You will hear a possible answer on the tape. First, listen to the list.

dar un paseo   visitar el Museo de Arte Moderno
hacer *camping*   divertirse en el parque
jugar a las cartas   tomar el sol

1. ...   2. ...   3. ...   4. ...   5. ...   6. ...

B. *¿Qué están haciendo estas personas?* When you hear the corresponding number, tell what the following people might be doing, using the present progressive. You will hear a possible answer on the tape.

1.

3.

2.

4.

C. *Conversación: La vida de la gran ciudad.* You will hear a conversation, partially printed in your manual, about leisure-time activities in the city. Then you will participate in a similar conversation. Complete it based on the cues suggested. You will hear a possible answer on the tape.

—¿Cómo pasas tus ratos libres aquí en la capital?

—A veces _____

—¿No te gusta visitar los museos?

— _____

Here are the cues for your conversation:

caminar por el parque o tomar el sol
no gustar / el arte / preferir / ir al teatro

Pronunciación y ortografía: Repaso

Read the following sentences, paying close attention to linking, rhythm, and intonation. Then repeat each sentence after you hear it.

1. ¡Ésta es una finca hermosa (*beautiful*)!
   Este invierno es necesario que conservemos energía.
   Quiero que apagues las luces cuando salgas del baño.
2. Estás aburrida.
   ¿Estás aburrida?
   ¿Por qué estás aburrida?
3. Nos mandaron una invitación.
   ¿Nos mandaron una invitación?
   ¿Quiénes nos mandaron una invitación?
4. ¡Qué sorpresa! ¿Cuándo llegaste?
   Me sorprendí cuando supe que llegaste.
   ¿Quién se sorprendió cuando llegaste?

Estructuras

42. Influencing Others: **Tú** Commands

A. *Minidiálogo: En la escuela primaria: Frases útiles para la maestra.* You will hear a dialogue followed by a series of statements. Circle the letter of the person who might have made each statement.

1. a) una alumna   b) la maestra   3. a) una alumna   b) la maestra
2. a) una alumna   b) la maestra   4. a) una alumna   b) la maestra

B. *Un viaje en el coche de Raúl.* Form new sentences, using the oral cues.

1. —Raúl maneja muy mal. ¿Qué le pide Ud.? (no arrancar rápidamente) →
   —Raúl, <u>no arranques rápidamente</u>.

   a. ...   b. ...   c. ...

2. —Cuando el coche no funciona, ¿qué le dice Ud. a Raúl? (revisar el motor) →
   —<u>Revisa el motor,</u> Raúl.

   a. ...   b. ...   c. ...

C. *Consejos.* Your friend Estela is about to do the following things. Advise her what to do, or what *not* to do, using informal commands based on verbs from the following list. Add any other necessary information. You will hear a possible answer on the tape. First, listen to the list.

(no) comer tanto/a _____   (no) tomar _____ (*curso*)

(no) llevar _____ al taller   (no) quejarse con _____

     MODELO: (Me faltan dos cursos de idiomas para graduarme y no sé cuáles tomar.) →
                Pues, toma el francés tres y una clase de conversación.

1. ...   2. ...   3. ...   4. ...

Estructuras

43. ¿Hay alguien que...? ¿Hay un lugar donde... ? Subjunctive After Nonexistent and Indefinite Antecedents

A. *En la plaza central.* You will hear a series of statements about the drawing. Circle *C* if the statement is true or *F* if it is false. First, look at the drawing.

1. C F   2. C F   3. C F   4. C F

B. *¿Sabe Ud. jugar al ajedrez?* You will hear a series of sentences. Each will be said twice. Circle the appropriate letters to indicate whether the sentence refers to a known or to an as yet unknown person.

1. a) known   b) unknown   3. a) known   b) unknown
2. a) known   b) unknown   4. a) known   b) unknown

C. *En busca de una casa nueva.* Form new sentences, using the oral cues.

1. —¿Qué tipo de casa buscan Uds.? (estar en el campo) →
   —Buscamos una casa que <u>esté en el campo</u>.

    a. ...   b. ...   c. ...   d. ...

2. —Y ¿cómo quieren Uds. que sean los vecinos? (jugar a las cartas) →
   —Queremos vecinos que <u>jueguen a las cartas</u>.

    a. ...   b. ...   c. ...   d. ...

Un poco de todo

A. *Dictado: El viernes por la noche.* You will hear a brief theater ad, followed by a brief conversation. Each will be read twice. Listen carefully and write the requested information. First, listen to the list of information. Listening first will give you an idea of what to listen for.

cuándo tiene lugar la función _____

el nombre de la comedia _____

la actriz principal_____

el nombre del teatro _____

el nombre de las personas que van a la función _____ ,

_____ y _____

B. *¿Qué tienen estas personas? Y ¿qué desean?* When you hear the corresponding number, tell what these people have and what they want, using the written cues. You will hear a possible answer on the tape.

MODELO: viejo / nuevo →
<u>Arturo tiene un auto (que es) viejo; desea uno que sea nuevo.</u>

1. no tener vista / tener vista

2. perezoso / trabajador

3. grande / pequeño

4. hacer mucho ruido / ser más tranquilos

C. *Entrevista: Hablando de pasatiempos.* You will hear a series of questions. Each will be said twice. Answer based on your own experience. No answers will be given on the tape. (If you prefer, stop the tape and write the answer.)

1. _____

2. _____

3. _____

4. _____

5. _____

6. _____

D. *Y para terminar...Una canción.* **Cu cu ru cu cu** is a traditional Mexican folk song.

Cu cu ru cu cu

Dicen que por las noches no más se le iba° en puro llorar.   no... pasaba su tiempo
Dicen que no comía, no más se le iba en puro tomar.
Juran que el mismo cielo se estremecía al oír su llanto.°   Juran... *They swear that*
Cómo sufría por ella, que hasta en su muerte la fue llamando: *even the heavens were*
Ay, ay, ay, ay, ay, cantaba.   *touched by his grief.*
Ay, ay, ay, ay, ay, gemía.°   *he moaned*
Ay, ay, ay, ay, ay, cantaba.
De pasión mortal moría.
Cu cu ru cu cu,
cu cu ru cu cu,
cu cu ru cu cu.
Paloma,° ya no le llores.   *Dove*

Un paso más: Situaciones

A. *¿Qué quieres hacer?* You will hear two conversations about activities. Read them silently, along with the speakers.

Un fin de semana en la ciudad

—¿Qué hacen Uds. los fines de semana?
—Nos encanta pasear por la mañana, cuando hay poco tráfico.
—Sí, y a veces visitamos alguna exposición de arte y después tomamos el aperitivo en un café.
—¿Me permiten ir con Uds. alguna vez?
—¡Encantados!

Delante del cine

—¡Hola, hombre! ¿Tú también vienes a ver *El Museo de Drácula?*
—¡Qué va! Voy a ver *El Sol de Acapulco.*
—¿Por qué no nos acompañas? Está con nosotros Marisa, la prima de Carlos.
—Lo siento, pero voy a encontrarme con Elena Ortega... y además a mí me parecen pesadísimas las películas de horror.
—Hasta luego, entonces. Que lo pases bien.
—Chau. Y ¡que se diviertan!

B. Now you will participate in a similar conversation, partially printed in your manual, about a summer afternoon activity. Complete it based on the cues suggested. No answers will be given on the tape.

Here are the cues for your conversation.

ir a la ciudad
dos semanas / ir al teatro / visitar el museo de arte
encantarnos las comedias y los cuadros (*paintings*) de Goya

—El mes que viene _____

—¿Cuánto tiempo piensan pasar allí?

—_____. Vamos a _____

—Eso es lo que más les gusta a Uds., ¿verdad?

—Sí, _____

Pues, ¡que se diviertan todos!

CAPÍTULO
22

Vocabulario: ¿Eres deportista?

A. *Definiciones:* You will hear a series of statements. Each will be said twice. Circle the letter of the word that is best defined by each.

1. a) la piscina   b) el traje de baño   4. a) la raqueta   b) la cancha
2. a) el golf   b) el fútbol   5. a) la red   b) el trofeo
3. a) el partido   b) el equipo   6. a) patinar   b) esquiar

B. *Descripción.* Tell what the following people are doing when you hear the corresponding numbers. Use the written cues. You will hear a possible answer on the tape.

1. patinar

los niños

3. pasear

Leonor

2. mirar

4. tirar (*to throw*)

yo

Estructuras

44. Expressing Contingency and Purpose: The Subjunctive After Certain Conjunctions

A. *Minidiálogo: Unos verdaderos aficionados.* You will hear a dialogue followed by a series of statements. Circle *C* if the statement is true of *F* if it is false. In this exercise, you will practice listening for specific information.

1. C F   2. C F   3. C F   4. C F

B. *Un viaje.* You will hear the following pairs of sentences. Then you will hear a conjunction. Join each pair of sentences, using the conjunction and making any necessary changes.

> MODELO: Hacemos el viaje. No cuesta mucho. (con tal que) →
> <u>Hacemos el viaje con tal que no cueste mucho</u>.

1. Tenemos que salir. Empieza a llover.
2. No queremos ir. Hace sol.
3. Pon las maletas en el coche. Podemos salir pronto.
4. Trae el mapa. Nos perdemos.

Now answer the questions you hear, based on your interpretation of the preceding sentences. Each will be said twice. You will hear a possible answer on the tape.

1. ...   2. ...   3. ...   4. ...

C. *Descripción.* Circle the letter of the picture best described by the sentences you hear. Each sentence will be said twice.

1. a)    b)

2. a)    b)

3. a)    b)

4. a)    b)

D. *¿Quién lo dijo?* When you hear the number, read each of the following statements, giving the present subjunctive form of the verbs in parentheses. You will hear the correct answer on the tape. Then you will hear the names of two different people. Circle the letter of the person who might have made each statement.

1. a b No les doy los paquetes a los clientes antes de que me (*pagar*).
2. a b Voy a revisar las llantas en caso de que (*necesitar*) aire.
3. a b No compro esa computadora a menos que (*ser*) fácil de manejar.
4. a b Voy a tomarle la temperatura al paciente antes de que lo (*ver*) la doctora.

Estructuras

45. More About Expressing Possession: Stressed Possessives

A. *Minidiálogo: En el club de tenis.* You will hear a dialogue followed by three statements. Circle the number of the statement that best summarizes the dialogue. In this exercise you will practice listening for the main idea.

1   2   3

B. *¿A qué se refiere?* You will hear a series of sentences containing stressed possessive pronouns. Circle the letter of the word to which the pronoun in each sentence might refer.

1. a) la pelota   b) las pelotas   4. a) los zapatos   b) las corbatas
2. a) los papeles   b) las cartas   5. a) los abrigos   b) el ordenador
3. a) el traje de baño b) la ropa

C. *Hablando de lo que nos pertenece* (belongs). Practice telling about some of your possessions, using the oral and written cues.

> MODELO: arreglado   (La computadora de Antonio está rota. ¿Y la tuya?)→
> ¿La <u>mía</u>? Ya <u>la</u> he <u>arreglado</u>.

1. arreglado   3. arreglado
2. llenado de aire   4. limpiado

D. *Preguntas: Comparaciones.* A friend from another university is describing his home and school environments. He then asks how they compare to your own. Each description will be said twice. Answer his questions according to the model. You will hear a possible answer on the tape.

> MODELO: (Hay 65.000 estudiantes en mi universidad. ¿Cuál es más grande, mi universidad o la
> tuya?) → <u>La tuya es más grande que la mía</u>.

1. ...   2. ...   3. ...   4. (horario = *schedule*)....

Un poco de todo

A. *Dictado: El día del partido.* You will hear three brief phone conversations, all about the same soccer game. You will hear each one only once. Listen carefully and write the requested information. First, listen to the list of information.

los nombres de los equipos que van a jugar _____

los nombres de las personas que van al partido _____

lo que no le gusta a Héctor _____

la hora que empieza el partido _____

lo que van a hacer Héctor y su amiga _____

B. *Listening Passage.* You will hear a brief passage about the movie industry in Hispanic countries. Then you will hear a series of statements about the passage. Circle *C* if the statement is true or *F* if it is false.

The following word appears in the passage: *premio* (*prize*).

1. C F   2. C F   3. C F   4. C F   5. C F

C. *Entrevista.* You will hear a series of questions about your hobbies and sports interests. Each will be said twice. Answer based on your own experience. No answers will be given on the tape. (If you prefer, stop the tape and write the answer.)

1. _____

2. _____

3. _____

4. _____

5. _____

D. *Y para terminar... Una canción.* "La casita" is a **ranchera**, a type of Mexican ballad or folk song.

La casita

¿Qué de dónde amigo vengo?
De una casita que tengo
más abajo del trigal;°   *más... below the wheat field*
de una casita chiquita,°   *muy pequeña*
para una mujer bonita
que me quiere acompañar.

Yedras° la tienen cubierta   *Ivy*
y un jazmín hay en la huerta°   *garden*
que las bardas ya cubrió,°   *que... that has already covered the fences*
en el portal° una hamaca,   *porch*
en el corral una vaca,°   *cow*
y adentro mi perro y yo.

Más adentro está la cama
muy olorosa a retama,°   *muy... smelling of broom*
limpiecita como usted;
tengo también un armario,°   *closet*
un espejo° y un canario   *mirror*
que en la feria me merqué.°   *me... compré*

Si usted quiere la convido°   *invito*
a que visite ese nido°   *nest*
que hay abajo del trigal.
Le echo la silla° a Lucero,   *Le... I'll saddle up*
que nos llevará ligero°   *quickly*
hasta en medio del jacal.°   *house, hut*

CAPÍTULO
23

Vocabulario: Las noticias

A. *El noticiero del Canal Diez*. You will hear a brief "newsbreak" from a television station. Then you will hear a series of statements about the newscast. Circle *C* if the statement is true or *F* if it is false.

1. C F   2. C F   3. C F   4. C F

B. *Definiciones*. You will hear a series of statements. Each will be said twice. Place the number of the statement next to the word that is best defined by each. First, listen to the list of words.

____ una guerra   ____ la testigo

____la prensa   ____ el reportero

____ un dictador   ____la huelga

____ los terroristas

C. *Dictado: Asociaciones*. You will hear several groups of words. Each group will be said twice. Write out the one word in each group that is *not* related and repeat it.

1. _____   3. _____

2. _____   4. _____

Estructuras

46. ¡Ojalá que pudiéramos hacerlo!: Past Subjunctive

A. *Minidiálogo: Aquéllos eran otros tiempos...* You will hear a brief dialogue and commentary, followed by a series of statements. Circle *C* if the statement is true or *F* if it is false.

VIEJOS VOTANTES.–¿Recuerda cuánto tuvimos que discurrir usted y yo antes de votar hace treinta años?

1. C F   2. C F   3. C F

B. *Recuerdos.* Form new sentences, using the oral cues.

1. —Cuando Ud. estudiaba en la secundaria, ¿qué le gustaba? (estudiar idiomas) →
   —Me gustaba que <u>estudiáramos idiomas</u>.

   a. ...   b. ...   c. ...   d. ...

2. —De niña, ¿cómo era su vida? (ser buena) →
   —Mis padres querían que <u>fuera buena</u>.

   a. ...   b. ...   c. ...   d. ...

C. *¿Qué pasó ayer en el almacén?* You will hear the following statements from store employees. Using the oral cues, restate each to express a past event.

   MODELO: No *quieren* que lo hagamos. (querían) → <u>No *querían* que lo hiciéramos</u>.

1. No *creo* que tengamos que trabajar tarde hoy.
2. Pero el jefe *insiste* en que nos quedemos hasta las ocho.
3. *Es* necesario que hagamos el inventario.
4. No *hay* nadie que esté contento con estas condiciones de trabajo.
5. Le *decimos* al jefe que *vamos* a hacer una huelga a menos que nos dé un aumento.

D. *¿Qué quería Ud.?* You are never happy with your family's plans. What would you have rather done? Use the written cues to tell what you preferred, beginning with **Yo quería que....**

   MODELO: (Ayer cenamos en el restaurante El Perico Negro.) en casa→
              <u>Yo quería que cenáramos en casa</u>.

1. comedia   4. computadora
2. campo   5. arroz
3. dar un paseo

E. *El noticiero del mediodía: Un informe especial.* You will hear a radio newscast. It will be read twice. Then you will hear a series of statements about the newscast. Circle *C* if the statement is true or *F* if it is false.

1. C F   2. C F   3. C F   4. C F

F. *Entrevista: Hablando del pasado.* You will hear a series of questions. Each will be said twice. Answer based on your own experience. You will hear a possible answer on the tape. (If you prefer, stop the tape and write the answer.)

1. _____

2. _____

3. _____

4. _____

5. _____

6. _____

Un poco de todo

A. *Dictado: Hablando de las elecciones.* You will hear a brief conversation between Alberto and Raquel. It will be read twice. Listen carefully and jot down the requested information in the spaces provided. First, listen to the list of requested information.

el nombre de la candidata que perdió las elecciones _____

el nombre del candidato que ganó las elecciones _____

el porcentaje (*percentage*) de los ciudadanos que votó por la candidata que perdió_____

la cuestión principal de la campaña _____

> **B.** *Estrategias: More on Word Families.* You have already practiced guessing the meanings of words related to other words you already know, that is, words that share a common root. Your knowledge of suffixes is also helpful in determining the meaning and part of speech of the unfamiliar yet related word. For example, you know that **contaminar** is a verb. In the word **contaminado**, the suffix **-ado** tells you immediatelythat this word is a past participle, equivalent to a verb form with an English *-ed* ending. In the word **contaminación**, the **-ión** suffix tells you that this word is a noun.

In this exercise, you will hear the same sentence several times. After each reading of the sentence, you will hear questions about a word in the sentence. Circle the letter of the correct answer. ¡OJO! There may be more than one.

1. a) arroyo   b) desarrollar   c) desordenado
2. a) un sustantivo   b) un adjetivo   c) un verbo
3. a) *-ty*   b) *-tion*   c) *-ly*
4. a) un sustantivo   b) un adjetivo   c) un adverbio
5. a) naturaleza   b) normales   c) naturalmente

C. *Descripción: Escenas actuales*. You will hear the following cartoon captions. Then you will hear a series of questions. Each will be said twice. Answer based on the cartoons and your own experience. You will hear a possible answer on the tape.

—Lo bueno de las campañas políticas es que no te las pueden repetir.

1. ...   2. ...   3. ...   4. ...

—No veáis mucha televisión... Dentro de tres crímenes y seis asaltos apagáis el aparato.

5. ...   6. ...   7. ...   8. ...

D. *Entrevista: Temas diversos.* You will hear a series of questions. Each will be said twice. Answer based on your own experience. No answers will be given on the tape. (If you prefer, stop the tape and write the answer.)

1. _____

2. _____

3. _____

4. _____

5. _____

6. _____

7. _____

8. _____

E. *Y para terminar... Una canción.* "Adelita" is a traditional Mexican song that originated during the Mexican Revolution.

Adelita

Si Adelita se fuera con otro,
La seguiría por tierra y por mar,
Si por mar en un buque° de guerra,   *boat*
Y por tierra en un tren militar.

Y si acaso yo muero en la guerra,
Y mi cuerpo en la tierra va a quedar,
Adelita, por Dios, te lo ruego
Que por mí no vayas a llorar.

Un paso más: Situaciones

A. *Hablando de las noticias.* You will hear two dialogues about world events. Read the dialogues silently, along with the speakers.

En la televisión

—¿Oíste lo del último accidente de aviación?
—¿Te refieres al accidente en que murieron cerca de 150 personas?
—Sí. Dicen que sucedió por pura negligencia.
—Es difícil creerlo, ¿no? Parece imposible que el piloto no pudiera hacer nada para evitarlo.
—Bueno, hay que tomar en cuenta que es posible que el avión tuviera un desperfecto.
—No creo que fuera eso.... Si las autoridades se interesaran más por proteger al público...
—Bueno. Es cuestión de opiniones. Personalmente creo que sí se interesan.
—¡Pero no lo suficiente! Yo creo que...

En el periódico

—¿Algo nuevo?
—¡Qué va! Centroamérica está a punto de estallar, la tensión sigue creciendo en el Golfo Pérsico, la situación en el Oriente Medio continúa igual de catastrófica...
—Ya veo. Lo de siempre.

B. Now you will participate in a conversation, partially printed in your manual, about the latest news. Complete it, based on the cues suggested. You will hear a possible answer on the tape.

Here are the cues for your conversation.

el noticiero del Canal Ocho
explotar otra bomba terrorista en Europa / haber muchos heridos (*wounded people*)

—¿Has oído _____

—No. ¿Qué pasó? Nada malo, espero.

—Pues, _____

— _____

CAPÍTULO

24

Vocabulario: En el banco

A. *Asuntos financieros.* You will hear a series of situations. Each will be described twice. Choose the most logical solution to each situation. ¡OJO! There may be more than one right answer.

1. a) Dejo de comprar cosas innecesarias.
    b) Gasto más en diversiones.
    c) Pongo más dinero en mi cuenta de ahorros.

2. a) Busco un compañero para compartir (share) el alquiler.
    b) Me mudo a un apartamento más caro.
    c) Me quejo con el gerente.

3. a) Me quejo con el departamento de créditos.
    b) Pago los $20,00 sin quejarme
    c) Les devuelvo el dinero.

4. a) Pago con dinero en efectivo.
    b) Pago con cheque.
    c) Uso mi tarjeta de crédito.

5. a) Pago con dinero en efectivo.
    b) Pago a plazos.
    c) Hablo con el cajero.

B. *Descripción.* You will hear a series of questions. Each will be said twice. Answer based on the drawing. You will hear a possible answer on the tape.

1. ...   2. ...   3. ...   4. ...   5. ...

C. *Dictado: Asociaciones.* You will hear several groups of words. Each group will be said twice. Write out the one word in each group that is not related and repeat it.

1. _____   3. _____

2. _____   4. _____

D. *En el periódico.* You will hear a brief ad for *el Grupo Banco Exterior de España.* Then you will hear two statements. Circle the number of the statement that best summarizes the ad.

PORTUGAL
BANCO EXTERIOR DE ESPAÑA
Oficina de Representación

Para trabajar en una Europa sin fronteras, usted necesita un banco sin fronteras.

El Banco Exterior de España es un experto en comercio internacional con todo el mundo y especialmente con la Europa Comunitaria.

Por eso, el Exterior tiene desde hace años una amplia red de bancos, sucursales y oficinas de representación en los países del Mercado Común.

Esta red y su experiencia en comercio exterior permiten al Grupo ofrecerle los conocimientos profesionales y la cobertura geográfica para hacer más fáciles y rápidas todas sus transacciones personales, profesionales y empresariales con los países de la CEE.

Olvide las fronteras, aproveche la conexión.

GRUPO BANCO EXTERIOR
El banco sin fronteras

1 2

E. *Conversación: Entre amigos.* You will hear a conversation, partially printed in your manual, about a loan. Then you will participate in a similar conversation about another kind of loan. Complete it based on the cues suggested. You will hear a possible answer on the tape.

—Oye, ¿ _____ ?

—¡Hombre! Bueno... si me los devuelves lo antes posible.

—Cómo no. _____ a más tardar (*at the latest*).

—¿Para qué necesitas tanto dinero?

— _____

Here are the cues for your conversation:

coche viejo
el lunes próximo
el mío / estar en el taller

Estructuras

47. Talking About the Future: Future Verb Forms

A. *Minidiálogo: ¡Hay que reducir los gastos! ¿Qué vamos a hacer?* You will hear a dialogue followed by a series of statements from the dialogue. Tell whether each statement would add to or reduce the family's expenses.

1. a) aumentar   b) reducir
2. a) aumentar   b) reducir
3. a) aumentar   b) reducir
4. a) aumentar   b) reducir

B. *Dictado: ¿Pretérito o futuro?* You will hear a series of sentences. Each will be said twice. Listen carefully and write the verbs you hear in the appropriate column.

PRETÉRITO	FUTURO
_____	_____
_____	_____
_____	_____

C. *El viernes por la tarde.* Using the oral and written cues, tell what the following people will do with their paychecks.

1. Bernardo   3. Adela y yo   5. yo
2. algunos empleados   4. tú... ¿verdad?

D. *El cumpleaños de Jaime.* Jaime's birthday is next week. Answer the questions about his birthday, using the written cues.

MODELO: (¿Cuántos años va a cumplir Jaime?) *dieciocho* → <u>Cumplirá dieciocho años</u>.

1. sus amigos y sus parientes   3. un pastel de chocolate   5. feliz cumpleaños
2. una grabadora de vídeo   4. discos

Estructuras

48. Expressing Future or Pending Actions: Subjunctive and Indicative After Conjunctions of Time

A. *Mafalda.* You will hear the caption for the following cartoon. Then you will hear a series of statements. Circle the letter of the person who might have made each statement.

1. a) Mafalda   b) el padre de Mafalda
2. a) Mafalda   b) el padre de Mafalda
3. a) Mafalda   b) el padre de Mafalda

B. *Dictado.* You will hear the following sentences. Each will be said twice. Write the missing words.

1. Voy a darte el dinero en cuanto _____ el cheque.

2. Nos llamarán tan pronto como _____.

3. Siempre comemos en un restaurante elegante cuando mis tíos nos _____

4. Anoche bailamos hasta que la orquesta _____ de tocar.

C. *Escenas de la vida cotidiana.* You will hear the following pairs of sentences. Combine them to form one complete sentence, using the oral cues.

> MODELO: Voy a decidirlo. Hablo con él. (despué de que) →
> <u>Voy a decidirlo después de que hable con él.</u>

1. Elisa se va a despertar. Oye el despertador.
2. No voy a estar contenta. Recibo un aumento.
3. Iba a mudarme a un apartamento. Mis padres vendieron su casa.
4. Comimos. Llegaron los niños. (¡OJO!)
5. Tito, apaga la luz. Has terminado.
6. Querían que les mandara una tarjeta postal. Yo salí del Perú.

D. *Descripción.* Tell what is happening in the following drawings by answering the questions. You will hear a possible answer on the tape.

MODELO: (¿Hasta cuándo va a esperar Ricardo?) →
<u>Hasta que llegue Gerardo.</u>

1.

2.

3.

4.

Un poco de todo

A. *Situaciones: ¿Qué cree Ud. que van a hacer estas personas?* You will hear three situations. Choose the most logical solution for each and repeat it.

1. a) Teresa comprará un coche barato y económico.
   b) Comprará un coche caro y lujoso.
   c) No comprará ningún coche.
2. a) Basilio tendrá que conseguir otro puesto para pagar el nuevo alquiler.
   b) Robará un banco.
   c) Compartirá (*He will share*) su apartamento con cuatro amigos.
3. a) Luisa empezará a poner el dinero que gasta en diversiones en su cuenta de ahorros.
   b) Les dirá a sus padres que no podrá comprarles un regalo este año.
   c) Insistirá en que su jefe le dé un aumento de sueldo inmediatamente.

B. *Listening Passage.* You will hear a brief passage about the **Banco Interamericano de Desarrollo (el BID)**. Then you will hear a series of statements about the passage. Circle **C** if the statement is true or **F** if it is false.

1. C F   2. C F   3. C F   4. C F

C. *Entrevista: Hablando del futuro.* You will hear a series of questions. Each will be said twice. Answer based on your own experience. No answers will be given on the tape. (If you prefer, stop the tape and write the answer.)

1. _____

2. _____

3. _____

4. _____

5. _____

D. *Y para terminar... Una canción.* The song "Cielito lindo" is popular throughout Hispanic America, and it is well known in some parts of the United States.

    Cielito lindo

De la Sierra Morena,
Cielito lindo,° vienen bajando,   *bonito*
Un par de ojitos negros,
Cielito lindo,
De contrabando.

Coro

Ay, ay, ay, ay,
Canta y no llores,
Porque cantando se alegran,
Cielito lindo,
Los corazones. (*bis*)

REPASO

6

A. *¿Dónde están estas personas?* You will hear a series of brief conversations or parts of conversations. Write the number of each next to the location in which the conversation might be taking place. First, listen to the list of locations.

___ un estadio   ___ una cancha

___ una gasolinera   ___ un banco

___ un museo   ___ un teatro

B. *Estrategias: Repaso.* You will hear a series of words. Each will be said twice. Circle the letter of the word or words to which each word is related. ¡OJO! There may be more than one answer.

1. a) inglés   b) grueso   c) ingreso
2. a) gastar   b) gustar   c) gas
3. a) seguridad   b) seguramente   c) siguiente
4. a) dejo   b) densidad   c) dentro
5. a) visto   b) vivo   c) vivienda

C. *Hablando de ordenadores.* You will hear the following sentences. Form one complete sentence, using the oral cues. Follow the model.

MODELO: No compramos ese ordenador. Nos dan un buen precio. (a menos que) →
          <u>No compramos ese ordenador a menos que nos den un buen precio.</u>

1. No compres esa impresora. Te enseñan a usarla.
2. Mándame uno de tus discos. Puedo copiarlo.
3. Voy a editar los textos. Compro un nuevo programa.
4. No salgas esta tarde. Llama la técnica.

D. *¿De quién son estas cosas?* You will hear a series of questions. Answer in the negative, using the written cues to complete your answer.

MODELO: (¿El libro es de Jacinta?) más viejo → <u>No, no es suyo. El suyo es más viejo.</u>

1. extranjero   3. de lana   5. de dos pisos y está en el campo
2. negros   4. para balcón

E. *Opiniones.* You will hear a series of statements that describe the world today. React to each, using the written cues. ¡OJO! You will be using present subjunctive, present indicative, or past subjunctive verb forms.

MODELO: (Hay tantas guerras en el mundo.) es lástima →
          <u>Es lástima que haya tantas querras en el mundo.</u>

1. No dudo...   4. Es increíble...
2. No creemos...   5. No les gustaba a los políticos...
3. Era probable...   6. Es verdad...

F. *Dictado: El noticiero del mediodía* (noon). You will hear a radio newscast. Listen carefully and write down the requested information. First, listen to the list of information.

la fecha del noticiero _____

el tiempo que hace _____

el nombre de la fábrica donde terminó la huelga _____

lo que decidió darles a los obreros el dueño de la fábrica _____

_____

la fecha en que regresan al trabajo los obreros _____

el mes en que se jugará el campeonato _____

la temperatura alta durante los próximos tres días _____

G. *Conversación: Haciendo planes.* You will hear a conversation, partially printed in your manual, about plans for an afternoon. Then you will participate in a similar conversation. Complete it based on the cues suggested. No answers will be given on the tape.

—¡Qué _____ hace! ¿Qué te parece si _____ ?

—No, gracias. Prefiero quedarme en casa. _____ está puesto y la temperatura es perfecta aquí adentro.

—Como quieras (*As you wish*).... _____ , pues.

—¡Que te diviertas!

Here are the cues for your conversation:

frío / ir al Café Rioja a tomar un café
ir (yo) sin ti

H. *Descripción: Escenas actuales.* You will hear a series of questions. Each will be said twice. Answer based on the following cartoons and your own experience. You will hear a possible answer on the tape. First, listen to the cartoon captions.

1. ...   2. ...   3. ...   4. ...   5. ...   6. ...   7. ...

I. *Entrevista: Temas diversos.* You will hear a series of questions. Each will be asked twice. Answer based on your own experience. No answers will be given on the tape. (If you wish, stop the tape and write the answer.)

1. _____

2. _____

3. _____

4. _____

5. _____

6. _____

7. _____

8. _____

CAPÍTULO

25

Vocabulario: ¿En qué quieres trabajar?

A. *En busca de un puesto.* You are looking for a new job in a large corporation. Tell how you will go about getting the job, using phrases from the following list. First, listen to the list; then put the remaining items in order, from 3 to 6. Then when you hear the number, tell what you will do.

___ tratar de caerle bien al entrevistador

___ aceptar el puesto y renunciar a mi puesto actual (*present*)

_2_ pedirle una solicitud de empleo

___ ir a la entrevista

___ llenar la solicitud a máquina

_1_ llamar a la directora de personal

MODELO: 1. llamar a la directora de personal → Llamo a la directora de personal.

2. ...   3. ...   4. ...   5. ...   6. ...

B. *Dictado: Quejas de la oficina.* You overhear a series of statements coming from a closed-door meeting between management and employees. You will hear each statement twice. Listen carefully and write down the complaints in the appropriate blank.

Las quejas de los empleados:

1. _____

2. _____

3. _____

Las quejas de los jefes:

4. _____

5. _____

6. _____

C. *En el periódico: Empleos.* The following ads for jobs appeared in a Mexican newspaper. Choose the ad you are most interested in, based on the profession, and scan it. Answer the questions you hear, based on that ad. If the information requested is not in the ad, say **No lo dice.** No answers will be given on the tape. First, look at the ads and pick the one that interests you the most.

1. ...   2. ...   3. ...   4. ...   5. ...

Estructuras

49. Expressing What You Would Do: Conditional Verb Forms

A. *Minidiálogo: La fantasía de una maestra de primaria.* You will hear a teacher's description of how she would like her life to be. Then you will hear three statements. Circle the letter of the statement that best summarizes the teacher's description.

1
2
3

B. *¿Imperfecto o condicional?* You will hear a series of sentences. Each will be said twice. Circle the letter of the verb contained in each, imperfect or conditional.

1. a) imperfecto   b) condicional   4. a) imperfecto   b) condicional
2. a) imperfecto   b) condicional   5. a) imperfecto   b) condicional
3. a) imperfecto   b) condicional

C. *¿Qué harían para mejorar las condiciones?* Using the oral and written cues, tell what the following people would like to do to improve the world.

   MODELO: (Betty) eliminar las guerras → <u>Betty eliminaría las guerras</u>.

1. desarrollar otros tipos de energía   4. eliminar el hambre y las desigualdades
2. construir viviendas para todos   5. protestar por el uso de las armas atómicas
3. eliminar a los terroristas   6. matar a los dictadores

D. *Entrevista.* You will hear a series of questions. Each will be asked twice. Answer based on your own experience. No answers will be given on the tape. (If you prefer, stop the tape and write the answer.)

1. _____

2. _____

3. _____

4. _____

5. _____

Un poco de todo

A. *Estrategias: Repaso.* You will hear a brief passage that contains some unfamiliar words. It will be followed by a series of statements about the paragraph. Circle *C* if the statement is true, *F* if it is false, or **No lo dice** if the information is not in the passage. Before listening to the passage, listen to the following sentences. Try to guess the meaning of the underlined words.

- El Sr. Carrasco fue presidente de la compañía por 10 años. Mientras <u>desempeñaba</u> ese <u>cargo</u>, se efectuaron muchos cambios positivos.
- Para <u>desempeñara</u> bien el <u>cargo</u> de directora de personal, es necesario saber cómo entrevistar a las personas.

1. C   F   No lo dice
2. C   F   No lo dice
3. C   F   No lo dice

B. *¡Entendiste mal!* Make statements about your plans, using the written cues when you hear the corresponding numbers. Make any necessary changes or additions. When your friend Alicia misunderstands your statements, correct her. Follow the model.

MODELO: llegar / trece / junio →
        UD.: <u>Llegaré el trece de junio.</u>
    ALICIA: ¿No dijiste que llegarías el tres?
        UD.: <u>¡No, no, no! Te dije que llegaría el trece. Entendiste mal.</u>

1. estar / bar / doce
2. estudiar / Juan
3. ir / vacaciones / junio
4. verte / casa
5. tomar / tres / clases

C. *Listening Passage.* You will hear a brief passage about one aspect of the economic system of Latin America, **el pluriempleo.** Then you will hear a series of questions about the passage. Choose the best answer to each.

1. a) Es tener más de un empleo.
   b) Es trabajar por la noche.
2. a) Tendría que ser rico o ser un profesor eminente.
   b) Podría vivir bien sólo con el sueldo de profesor.
3. a) Predomina en la clase alta.
   b) Predomina en la clase baja y en la clase media.
4. a) Sí, corresponde al estereotipo del latino perezoso.
   b) No, no corresponde al estereotipo del latino perezoso.

D. *Entrevista: Hablando de puestos.* You will hear a series of questions. Each will be said twice. Answer based on your own experience. No answers will be given on the tape. (If you prefer, stop the tape and write the answer.)

1. _____
2. _____
3. _____
4. _____
5. _____
6. _____

E. *Y para terminar... Una canción.* The song "Las mañanitas" is a traditional song that is sung—very early in the morning—to a woman on her birthday.

Las mañanitas

Éstas son las mañanitas
Que cantaba el Rey° David   *King*
A las muchachas bonitas.
Se las cantaba así:

Despierta, mi bien,° despierta,   *mi... my dear*
Mira que ya amaneció.°   *it has dawned*
Ya los pajarillos° cantan,   *little birds*
La luna ya se metió.°   *se... disappeared*

Qué linda° está la mañana   *bonita*
En que vengo a saludarte.°   *to greet you*
Venimos todos con gusto°   *con... gladly*
Y placer a felicitarte.

Con jazmines y flores
Te venimos a cantar.
Levántate de mañana.
Mira, que ya amaneció.

Un paso más: Situaciones

A. *El mundo del trabajo.* You will hear two dialogues about jobs and careers. Read them silently, along with the speakers.

Hablando de la entrevista

—¿Qué tal te fue esta mañana?
—Pues, no sé qué decirte. Me dijeron que me avisarían en una semana. ¿Y a ti?
—Lo mismo, pero no creo que me lo den. Tenían mucho interés en la experiencia que pudieran tener los candidatos, y como sabes, no tengo ninguna.

Hablando con los amigos

—¡Hola¡ ¿Ya tienes trabajo?
—¡Qué más quisiera! Me gustaría trabajar en lo mío, pero de momento no hay nada.
—Por lo visto los futuros biólogos no interesan demasiado...
—Hombre, a veces pienso que si volviera a entrar en la universidad, cambiaría de carrera, porque voy a tardar en colocarme de biólogo.
—Pues, no es sólo en lo tuyo. No sé si te acuerdas, pero yo tardé medio año en colocarme. ¡Y ahora llevo siete meses trabajando! O sea, ¡ánimo!

B. *Hablando con el entrevistador.* Now you will participate in an interview in which the director of personnel is interviewing you for a job in your field, **su campo.** Listen carefully; you will hear each question only once. Answer based on your own experience. No answers will be given on the tape.

1. ...   2. ...   3. ...   4. ...   5. ...   6. ...

CAPÍTULO

26

Vocabulario: Profesiones y oficios

A. *¿A quién necesitan en estas situaciones?* You will hear a series of situations. Circle the letter of the person or professional who would best be able to help. Do not be distracted by unfamiliar vocabulary; concentrate instead on the main idea of each situation.

1. a) un arquitecto
2. a) una dentista
3. a) una consejera matrimonial
4. a) una fotógrafa
5. a) un plomero

   b) un carpintero
   b) una enfermera
   b) un policía
   b) un bibliotecario
   b) una electricista

B. *¿Quiénes son?* Using the list of professions below, identify these people after you hear the corresponding number. Begin each sentence with **Es un...** or **Es una....** First, listen to the list of professions.

obrero/a
peluquero/a
periodista
veterinario/a

cocinero/a
fotógrafo/a
plomero/a
hombre o mujer de negocios

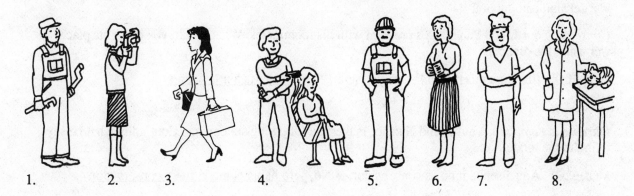

1.   2.   3.   4.   5.   6. 7.   8.

Estructuras

50. Expressing Hypothetical Situations: *What if... ?*: Conditional Sentences

A. *Minidiálogo: Una entrevista en la dirección del Canal 45.* You will hear a dialogue followed by a series of statements. Circle *C* if the statement is true or *F* if it is false.

1. C   F
2. C   F
3. C   F

B. *Situaciones.* You will hear three brief situations. Circle the letter of the best reaction to each.

1. a) ...regresaría a casa en autobús   b) ...llamaría a la policía inmediatamente
2. a) ...escribiría un cheque   b) ...me ofrecería a lavar los platos
3. a) ...trataría de negociar con el líder   b) ...despediría a todos los empleados
        del sindicato laboral

C. *Consejos.* Your friend Pablo has a problem with his roommates. What would you do in his place? Answer using the oral cues.

MODELO: (llamar a mis padres) → Si yo fuera Pablo, <u>llamaría a mis padres</u>.

1. ...   2. ...   3. ...   4. ...

D. *Durante la campaña.* Your friend Nicanor makes the following statements. Contradict what he says, according to the model.

MODELO: Aquel senador no es conservador.→ No, <u>pero habla como si fuera conservador</u>.

1. El candidato Molina no cree en los derechos humanos.
2. El gobernador no protege el medio ambiente.
3. Al gobernador no le interesan los problemas de los inmigrantes.
4. Ese candidato no toma en cuenta la opinión de las mujeres.

E. *Las finanzas.* You will hear the following sentences. Restate each, using the conditional.

MODELO: No le ofrecerán el puesto a menos que tenga buenas recomendaciones. →
          <u>Le ofrecerían el puesto si tuviera buenas recomendaciones</u>.

1. No le harán el préstamo a menos que esté trabajando.
2. No ahorraré más dinero a menos que controle mis gastos.
3. No pagaré las cuentas antes de que reciba el cheque semanal.
4. No te cobrarán el cheque hasta que lo firmes.

Un poco de todo

A. *¿Qué haría Ud.?* Tell what you would do in these locations when you hear the corresponding number. You will hear a possible answer on the tape.

MODELO: → <u>Si estuviera en la biblioteca, leería un libro.</u>

1.

2.  3.

4.  5.

B. *Listening Passage.* You will hear a brief passage about people who migrate in search of jobs. Then you will hear a series of statements about the passage. Circle *C* if the statement is true or *F* if it is false.

1. C F   2. C F   3. C F   4. C F

C. *En el periódico: Empleos.* You will hear three job ads from Hispanic newspapers. Write the number of the ad next to the name of the person who might want the job. First, listen to the list of candidates.

____ Ricardo es carpintero. Siempre le ha gustado hacer cosas de madera. El año pasado le hizo un estante muy bonito a su madre. También ha hecho otros muebles.

____ Sabrina sabe hablar español, inglés y alemán. También sabe escribir a máquina y usar una computadora. Es una persona muy eficiente y organizada.

____ Julia ha trabajado en la industria petrolera por ocho años. Es ingeniera, pero también ha tenido a su cargo la planeación de proyectos y el análisis de su costo.

D. *Entrevista: Hablando de posibilidades.* You will hear a series of questions. Each will be said twice. Answer based on your own experience. No answers will be given on the tape. (If you prefer, stop the tape and write the answer.)

1. _____

2. _____

3. _____

4. _____

5. _____

E. *Y para terminar... Una canción.* "De colores" is a song from the Chicano tradition in the United States.

De colores

De colores, de colores se visten los campos°   *fields*
   en la primavera.
De colores, de colores son los pajaritos que
   vienen de fuera.
De colores, de colores es el arco iris° que   *arco... rainbow*
   vemos lucir°   *shine*
Y por eso los grandes amores de muchos
   colores me gustan a mí. (*bis*)

Canta el gallo,° canta el gallo con el quiri,   *rooster*
   quiri, quiri, quiri, quiri.
La gallina,° la gallina con el cara, cara,   *hen*
   cara, cara, cara.
Los polluelos,° los polluelos con el pío,   *chicks*
   pío, pío, pío, pí.
Y por eso los grandes amores de muchos
   colores me gustan a mí. (*bis*)

CAPÍTULO
27

Vocabulario: En un viaje al extranjero

A. *Definiciones.* You will hear a series of definitions. Each will be said twice. Write the number of the definition next to the word or phrase that is best defined by each. First, listen to the list of words and phrases.

___ viajar a otro país   ___ una multa

___ la planilla de inmigración   ___ la frontera

___ la nacionalidad   ___ el pasaporte

B. *Descripción.* Describe what these people are doing, using the verbs you will hear. You will hear a possible answer on the tape.

1. ...   2. ...   3. ...   4. ...   5. ...

Estructuras

51. ¿Por o para? A Summary of Their Uses

A. *Minidiálogo: Antes de aterrizar.* You will hear a dialogue followed by a series of statements. Circle *C* if the statement is true or *F* if it is false. You will practice listening for specific information.

1. C F   2. C F   3. C F   4. C F

B. *Reacciones.* You will hear a series of statements. Each will be said twice. Circle the letter of the most appropriate response to each.

1. a) ¿Por qué no lo llevamos a la sala   b) ¡Por fin!
de urgencias, por si acaso... ?
2. a) Pero por lo menos te mandó un regalo.   b) ¿Por ejemplo?
3. a) ¿Por ejemplo?   b) ¡Te digo que no, por última vez!
4. a) ¿Por qué tienes tanta sed?   b) Ah, por eso tienes tanta sed.
5. a) Por el aumento que acaban de darme.   b) Por dos horas.

C. *¿Para qué están Uds. aquí?* Using the oral and written cues, tell why the people mentioned are in these locations. First, listen to the list of reasons.

ingresar dinero en la cuenta de ahorros
hacer reservaciones para un viaje a Acapulco
celebrar nuestro aniversario
pedir un aumento de sueldo
conseguir todos los detalles de la situación
descansar y divertirse

> MODELO: ¿Para qué están los obreros en la dirección de personal?) →
> <u>Están allí para pedir un aumento de sueldo.</u>

1. ...   2. ...   3. ...   4. ...   5. ...

D. *¿Qué hacen estas personas?* Using **por**, tell what the following people are doing when you hear the corresponding number. You will hear a possible answer on the tape.

MODELO: → <u>Marcos habla por teléfono</u>.

1.

2.

3.

4.

5.

Un poco de todo

A. *Comentarios.* You will hear a series of descriptions or situations. Comment on each, using phrases chosen from the following list. Begin each answer with **Por eso....** Make any necessary changes or additions. First, listen to the list.

estudiar / ser: mecánica / maestra   ir / mercado / comprar: vino / Coca-Cola
caminar: parque / playa   correr: tarde / mañana
salir mañana: Aspen / Acapulco

MODELO: (A Alida siempre le ha gustado jugar con todo tipo de máquina. Desde que era muy joven
sabía arreglar relojes. tostadoras y otros aparatos pequeños.) →
<u>Por eso estudia para ser mecánica</u>.

1. ...   2. ...   3. ...   4. ...

B. *Listening Passage.* You will hear a brief passage about what you might see on a visit to Mexico. Then you will hear a series of statements about the passage. Circle *C* if the statement is true of *F* if it is false.

1. C   F   2. C   F   3. C   F   4. C   F

C. *En el periódico: Viajes.* The following ad appeared in a Mexican newspaper. You will hear a series of statements about the ad. Circle *C* if the statement is true or *F* if it is false. First, scan the ad.

VACACIONES...?

Venga con su familia al Hotel Riviera del Sol de Ixtapa y disfrute de un merecido descanso en las soleadas playas y tibias aguas del espléndido Pacífico Mexicano y ahorre con nuestros tradicionales:

RIVIERA PAQUETES...!!!

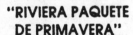

Vigencia: Julio 1º a Agosto 31, 1987

"RIVIERA PAQUETE DE PRIMAVERA"

3 NOCHES

4 DIAS

CON TRES DESAYUNOS

Precio por persona:
$ 80,000.00

Noche Extra:
$ 28,000.00

"PAQUETE MINI RIVIERA DE PRIMAVERA"

2 NOCHES

3 DIAS

CON DOS DESAYUNOS

Precio por persona:
$ 58,000.00

Noche Extra:
$ 28,000.00

1. C   F   2. C   F   3. C   F   4. C   F

D. *Entrevista.* You will hear a series of questions. Each will be said twice. Answer based on your own experience. No answers will be given on the tape. (If you prefer, stop the tape and write the answer.)

1. _____
2. _____
3. _____
4. _____
5. _____
6. _____
7. _____

E. *Y para terminar... Una canción.* The song "La llorona" is a song of lost love.

La llorona

Todos me dicen el negro, llorona,
Negro, pero cariñoso;   (bis)
Yo soy como el chile verde, llorona,
Picante,° pero sabroso.°   (bis) *Spicy / tasty*

Ay de mi llorona,
Llorona de ayer y hoy;   (bis)
Ayer maravilla° fui, llorona,   *marvel*
Y ahora ni sombra° soy.   (bis) ni... *not even a*
                                                                                                         shadow
Dicen que no tengo duelo,° llorona,   *sorrow*
Porque no me ven llorar:
Hay muertos que no hacen ruido, llorona,   (bis)
Y es más grande su penar.°   (bis) *pain*

Un paso más: Situaciones

A. *Viajando en el extranjero. En la aduana argentina.* You will hear a conversation between a traveler and a customs agent. Then you will hear a series of statements about the conversation. Circle *C* if the statement is true or *F* if it is false.

1. C F   2. C F   3. C F   4. C F

B. *Conversación: Pasando por la aduana.* You will hear a conversation, partially printed in your manual, between a customs inspector and a traveler. When it is read for the second time, take the role of the traveler and complete the conversation, based on the cues suggested. You will hear a possible answer on the tape.

INSPECTOR: ¿Cuál es su nacionalidad, por favor?

VIAJERO/A: _____

INSPECTOR: ¿Me da su pasaporte, por favor?

VIAJERO/A: Sí, cómo no. Aquí _____

INSPECTOR: ¿Tiene algo que declarar?

VIAJERO/A: Sí, compré _____ y _____ , pero son para uso personal.

INSPECTOR: Abra su maleta, por favor.

VIAJERO/A: Un momento, por favor. Se la _____

INSPECTOR: ¡Ud. tendrá que pagar una multa! Es ilegal llevar estas _____

VIAJERO/A: Lo siento... . De veras no sabía que era ilegal traer _____

                      ¿Cuánto es la multa?

INSPECTOR: Cuatrocientos pesos, por favor.

Here are the cues for your conversation:

canadiense / Toronto
blusa bordada a mano / par de zapatos
verduras

CAPÍTULO
28

Vocabulario: El alojamiento

A. *¿Un hotel de lujo o una pensión pequeña?* You will hear a series of statements. Each will be said twice. Circle the letter of the place that is best described by each.

1. a) un hotel de lujo   b) una pensión pequeña
2. a) un hotel de lujo   b) una pensión pequeña
3. a) un hotel de lujo   b) una pensión pequeña
4. a) un hotel de lujo   b) una pensión pequeña
5. a) un hotel de lujo   b) una pensión pequeña
6. a) un hotel de lujo   b) una pensión pequeña

B. *Preguntas.* You will hear a series of questions. Answer using words chosen from the following list. Make any necessary changes or additions to complete your answers. First, listen to the list.

propina   cheques de viajero
pensión   confirmar
huésped   recepción

1. ...   2. ...   3. ...   4. ...   5. ...   6. ...

C. *Conversación: En la recepción.* You will hear a conversation, partially printed in your manual, about getting a hotel room. Then you will participate in a similar conversation about another hotel. Complete it based on the cues suggested. You will hear a possible answer on the tape.

—¿Cuál es la tarifa de una habitación _____

—¿Con _____

—Con _____

—_____ pesos la noche, señor.

—Está bien. Quisiéramos quedarnos _____

—Muy bien, señor. Me hace el favor de firmar aquí y de enseñarme su pasaporte.

Here are the cues for your conversation:

media pensión
almuerzo y cena, por favor
cuatro noches

Preparaciones para un año en el extranjero

A. Listen to the following paragraph; then read it in the pause provided. You may want to record your reading.

Madrid, 7 de marzo

Querido Joe,

¡Cuánto me alegro de que por fin te hayas animado a escribirme y más todavía por eso que me cuentas de que tal vez te decidas a pasar un año en España! ¡Me parece genial! Has mejorado mucho tu español en estos últimos meses y, desde luego, un año en mi país sería perfecto.

B. *Cambiando dinero en un banco.* You will hear two dialogues about changing money in a foreign country. Read the dialogues silently, along with the speakers.

Al entrar

—Por favor. Quisiera cambiar moneda.
—Pase a la ventanilla 14, donde pone Cambio.
—Gracias, ¿eh?
—De nada.

Hablando con el cajero

—Sí, dígame. ¿Qué desea?
—Quisiera cambiar unos cheques de viajero en dólares a pesetas.
—¿Cuántos dólares quiere cambiar?
—Doscientos dólares, por favor. ¿A cuánto está el cambio hoy?
—A ciento veinte. ¿Ya firmó los cheques?
—Sí.
—Su pasaporte, por favor.
—Aquí lo tiene.
—Pase Ud. a la Caja con este recibo. La llamarán por este número.
—Y ¿cuándo me devuelven el pasaporte?
—En la Caja, señorita.

C. Now you will participate in a similar conversation, partially printed in your manual, about exchanging a different amount of money. Complete the conversation, based on the cues suggested. You will hear a possible answer on the tape. ¡OJO! The cues are not in sequence.

Here are the cues for your conversation:

querer cambiar estos cheques de viajero a pesetas
gracias
sí, aquí tenerlos (Ud.)
mil dólares / ¿a cuánto está el cambio?

—¿En qué puedo servirle?

— _____

—¿Cuántos dólares desea cambiar?

— _____ · ¿_____

—A ciento sesenta y uno. ¿Ya firmó los cheques?

— _____

—Déme su pasaporte, por favor, y pase a la Caja con este recibo. Allí lo llamarán por este número; le devolverán su pasaporte y le darán el dinero.

— _____

D. *Descripción: ¿Unos discos estupendos?* You will hear a series of questions. Each will be said twice. Answer based on the following cartoon. You will hear a possible answer on the tape. As you look at the cartoon and listen to the questions, keep in mind that the tourist in the drawing wants to go to Kiland, an imaginary country where Kiland is spoken. First, look at the cartoon.

1. ... 2. ... 3. ... 4. ... 5. ... 6. ...

E. *Entrevista final.* You will hear a series of questions or situations followed by questions. Each will be said twice. Answer based on your own experience. Model answers will be given on the tape for the last two questions. (If you prefer, stop the tape and write the answer.)

1. _____

2. _____

3. _____

4. _____

5. _____

6. _____

F. *Y para terminar... Una canción.* "Triste y sola" a is a traditional song sung by Spanish university students.

Triste y sola

Triste y sola,
Sola se queda Fonseca.
Triste y llorosa°   *tearful*
Queda la Universidad.
Y los libros,
Y los libros empeñados°   *pawned, in hock*
En el monte,°   montaña
En el monte de piedad.°   *pity*

No te acuerdas cuando te decía
A la pálida luz de la luna:
«Yo no puedo querer más que a una,
Y esa una, mi vida, eres tú.»

Triste y sola... (*bis*)

APPENDIX: ANSWERS TO **DICTADO** EXERCISES

Paso uno   C, Page 4

1. pesimista
2. inteligente
3. sincero
4. eficiente
5. sentimental

Paso dos: B, Page 5

1. Italia
2. piano, clarinete
3. dentista, turista
4. tigre
5. radio, bomba

Paso dos: D, Page 6

1. paso
2. casa
3. mesa
4. cine
5. pesar
6. misa

Paso dos: C, Page 7

6 seis; 13 trece; 24 veinticuatro; 2 dos; 0 cero; 3 tres; 28 veintiocho; 12 doce

Paso tres: B, Page 10

1. ¿Dónde está?
2. ¿Quién es el estudiante?
3. ¿Qué es esto?
4. ¿Cuánto es el chocolate?
5. ¿A qué hora es la excursión?
6. ¿Cuál es la capital?

Capítulo 1:   E, Page 17

1. Alicia es estudiante.
2. Pili está en el edificio.
3. ¿Cómo está usted?
4. Hay veintisiete estudiantes en clase hoy.

Capítulo 1:   D, Page 18

Personas: un dependiente, una mujer, un secretario
Edificios o lugares: una residencia, un hotel, una universidad
Cosas: una mochila, un bolígrafo, una mesa

Capítulo 1:   A, Page 18

Singular: el escritorio, un bolígrafo, un cuaderno
Plural: unos lápices, unos papeles, las sillas, unos libros

Capítulo 2:   C, Page 23

1. papá
2. música
3. práctico

4. nación
5. doctor
6. María

7. joven
8. inteligente
9. biología

Capítulo 2:   C, Page 24

ella: habla
nosotras: practicamos, Deseamos
yo: Trabajo, Tomo

Capítulo 3:   A, Page 30

cuarenta y cinco mochilas, noventa y nueve lápices, cincuenta y dos cuadernos, setenta y cuatro novelas, treinta y una calculadoras, cien libros de texto

Capítulo 4:   D, Page 39

1. Esta, aquel
2. Estos

3. Esa, aquella
4. esto

Capítulo 4:   B, Page 39

La hora de la boda: a las seis de la tarde
Los nombres de los esposos: Luisa Escalera Gallegos y Roberto Ramos Díaz
¿Hubo recepción después de la boda? Sí

Capítulo 5:   B, Page 48

1. Tomás también bebe cerveza.
2. Es bueno vivir aquí en Venezuela.
3. La abuela de Belinda es baja.
4. El abrigo es verde y la corbata es blanca.

Capítulo 6:   B, Page 54

1. cuatro
2. quince

3. cálculo
4. compras

5. parque
6. rico

Capítulo 6: A, Page 57

el nombre del almacén: el Almacén Carrillo
el precio de los zapatos para señora: veinte dólares
el precio de los trajes para caballero: cien dólares
tres cosas para el hogar: estéreos, radios, refrigeradores (sillas, sofás, computadoras...)
el precio del estéreo: novecientos dólares
el precio del sofá: trescientos dólares

Capítulo 7: B, Page 65

1. mejor, más de
2. tantos, menos de, menor
3. más, más de

Capítulo 9: D, Page 78

1. Don Guillermo es viejo y generoso.
2. Por lo general, los jóvenes de hoy son inteligentes.
3. El consejero de los estudiantes extranjeros es de Gijón.
4. Juana estudia geografía y geología.

Capítulo 10: D, Page 84

1. El cumpleaños de Begoña es mañana.
2. La señorita Marañón estudia mucho.
3. Esa muchacha es chilena.
4. Los señores Ibáñez son los dueños del Hotel España.

Capítulo 10: D, Page 87

1. deciden	2. cenar	3. es	4. Julio
5. mexicano	6. porque	7. esposo	8. él
9. gusta	10. llegan	11. les	12. mesa
13. les	14. demasiado	15. orquesta	16. está
17. mejor	18. le	19. al	20. leerlo
21. le	22. quieren	23. les	24. Después
25. le	26. pastel	27. al	28. los
29. cuenta	30. pagar	31. gustaría	32. cumpleaños

Capítulo 11: D, Page 93

1. El inspector quiere que los turistas le den los pasaportes.
2. Paquita y yo queremos que vengas con nosotros.
3. El señor Hurtado quiere que su esposa juegue al tenis.
4. Antonio quiere que naveguemos en un barco.

Repaso 3:   E, Page 103

el tipo de boleto: ida y vuelta
la fecha de salida: el 12 de noviembre
la fecha de regreso: el 28 de noviembre
la sección y la clase: sección de fumar, primera clase
la ciudad de la cual va a salir: Chicago
el tipo de hotel: en la playa, con aire acondicionado
el nombre del hotel: el Presidente

Capítulo 13:   B, Page 108

1. Hay muchos carteles en la pared.
2. El grabador de vídeo está encima del estante.
3. La mesita está a la izquierda de la cama.
4. La cocina no está limpia ahora.

Capítulo 13:   Page 111

1. práctico
2. acuarela
3. almacenista, almacenar
4. pescadores, pescar

Capítulo 14:   A, Page 116

1. ¿Cuál es tu profesión? ¿Te pagan bien?
2. Tú no la conoces, ¿verdad?
3. ¿Prefiere Ud. que le sirva la comida en el patio?
4. ¡Qué ejercicio más facil!
5. No sé dónde viven, pero sí sé su número de teléfono.

Capítulo 15:   C, Page 122

1. jugó
2. jugo
3. describes
4. descríbemela
5. sicología
6. sicólogo
7. almacén
8. almacenes
9. levántate
10. levanta
11. gusto
12. gustó

Capítulo 16:   B, Page 129

1. que, este, mí
2. está, tu, té, Qué
3. Él, que, te
4. Sí, mi, se

Capítulo 16:   B, Page 132

1. muy
2. enfermo
3. tenía
4. fiebre
5. me
6. dolía
7. mareado
8. respirar
9. empecé
10. toser
11. lo
12. peor
13. todo
14. cuerpo
15. hice
16. médico
17. me
18. recetó
19. antibiótico
20 tuve
21. guardar
22. cama
23. falté
24. semana
25. comí
26. bien
27. Esta
28. me
29. siento
30. mejor
31. enfermar

Capítulo 17:   B, Page 140

1. fosfato
2. atención
3. amoníaco
4. teología
5. oposición
6. fotografía
7. colección
8. arquitecto

Capítulo 17:   A, Page 142

1. se les olvidó
2. se le perdieron
3. se nos quede
4. se les rompieron

Capítulo 20:   B, Page 159

1. Me mudé al campo recientemente.
2. No me gustaban el ruido y el tráfico de la ciudad.
3. Ahora puedo vivir tranquilamente.
4. Visito la ciudad cuanto tengo ganas de ir al teatro.

Capítulo 21:   A, Page 170

cuándo tiene lugar la función: el viernes doce de abril a las nueve de la noche
el nombre de la comedia: Sol de invierno
la actriz principal: Corazón Aguilar
el nombre del teatro: el Teatro Nacional
el nombre de las personas que van a la función: Marta, Mercedes, Roberto

Capítulo 22:   A, Page 176

los nombres de los equipos: los Jefes y las Panteras
los nombres de las personas: Ricardo y Teresa
lo que no le gusta a Héctor: los deportes
la hora que empieza el partido: a las siete de la noche
lo que van a hacer Héctor y su amiga: ir al cine

Capítulo 23:   C, Page 179

1. los demás
2. la dictadura

3. la esperanza
4. ofrecer

Capítulo 23:   A, Page 181

el nombre de la candidata que perdió las elecciones: Quejada
el nombre del candidato que gano las elecciones: Muñoz
el porcentaje de los cindadanes que votó por la candidata que perdió: 30% (treinta por ciento)
la cuestión principal de la campaña: la educación pública

Capítulo 24:   C, Page 185

1. quejarse
2. el alquiler

3. gastar
4. el sueldo

Capítulo 24:   B, Page 187

Pretérito: presté, se enojó, devolví
Futuro: aprenderá, pagaremos, podré

Capítulo 24:   B, Page 188

1. cobre
2. pueden

3. visitan
4. dejó

Repaso 6:   F, Page 192

la fecha del noticiero: el lunes, ocho de enero
el tiempo que hace: está nevando, hace frío
el nombre de la fábrica donde terminó la huelga: Barrera
lo que decidió darles a los obreros el dueño de la fábrica: un pequeño aumento de sueldo
la fecha en que regresan al trabajo los obreros: el quiíce de enero
el mes en que se jugará el campeonato: febrero
la temperatura alta durante los próximos tres días: 20 grados Fahrenheit

Capítulo 25:   B, Page 195

Las quejas de los empleados:
1. Siempre dicen que somos perezosos.
2. Nunca nos dan los aumentos que pedimos.
3. Creo que ellos ganan mucho más que nosotros.

Las quejas de los jefes:
4. Nunca llegan a tiempo.
5. Siempre quieren que les demos un aumento.
6. Nunca quieren quedarse a trabajar después de las cinco.